"She's been through more hell than you'll ever know. But that's what gives her beauty an edge ... You can't touch a woman who can wear pain like the grandest of diamonds around her neck."

—Alfa (c)

"I sincerely believe that chemoradiation for head and neck cancer is the most challenging medical ordeal a person can endure. It stresses the body, the mind, and the soul to degrees that are difficult to truly communicate or conceptualize. It was an honor and a privilege to observe Ilse through her journey. Her strength, humor, graciousness, and spirit were inspiring to me and all who encountered her during and after her journey. This book is an excellent testament to the capacity of human spirit."

—**Dr. Eric S. Nadler, MD**
Medical Oncology

"Great to be inspired by Ilse."

—**Sergio Nicolau**
President and Executive Producer, Milagro Films

"*Say Yes to Life* exudes the indispensable quality that describes Ilse Anderson. To have been a part of her extraordinary spiritual and healing journey has been remarkable. What an inspiring story. What an honor to call her my friend."

—**Lupita Gurule de Martinez**
Owner, Pamper the Spirit, LLC,
Nurture the Soul, Santa Fe, New Mexico

"'You have to live, live, live!' said Auntie Mame. 'Life is a banquet and most poor suckers are starving to death.' Ilse Anderson is doing just that. Before cancer, Ilse lived her life to the fullest. Post cancer, she is absolutely soaring. Applause, applause, applause."

—Rebecca Koven
Precious Jewelry Designer, New York, NY

"As a believer in the concept that 'as long as we have breath, we have a purpose,' it is no accident that Ilse's brilliance and resiliency has been revealed through an unexpected hurdle late in life. Her beautifully written book will inspire you to clutch life, and all that it offers, for what it can teach us."

—Kristin S. Kaufman
President, Alignment, Inc., Social Commerce Entrepreneur Business Leadership Consultant, Portfolio Business Owner, Speaker, and Author of the highly acclaimed *Is This Seat Taken?* book series

"Coco Chanel once said, 'Elegance is refusal.' I have always admired Ilse's extreme poise when faced with emotionally charged and difficult life situations. When she found herself facing the biggest challenge of her life, she refused to give up. Her story is proof that having an optimistic attitude can impact the outcome. Well done."

—Cathy Brittingham Saxon
Dallas, TX

Say Yes to Life

ILSE ANDERSON

Clovercroft/Publishing

Say Yes to Life

©2017 by Ilse Anderson

Published by Clovercroft Publishing, Franklin, Tennessee

Published in association with Larry Carpenter of Christian Book Services, LLC of Franklin, Tennessee

Cover Design by Omar Mediano

Interior design by Adept Content Solutions

Edited by Christy Calahan

ISBN: 978-1-945507-48-9

Printed in the United States of America

For Aina, Andie, Paul, and Titan,
With all my love.

Contents

Preface

L ife is a journey and a precious gift. If we allow ourselves to live it fully, with all its joys and challenges, we
embark on an adventure that will change us in countless
ways as we evolve.

The most interesting people have faced many difficulties.
They have been buffeted by storms, but they hold steadfast
and keep moving forward. These people rarely talk about
their troubles, preferring instead to live in the present,
where they stay open to new people and experiences. They
love themselves and life—and it shows. Look at anyone
who lives life fully. Their eyes are aglow with what the
French call "joie de vivre" (joy of living).

As I faced the cancer monster, I had to believe in myself
and my power to get my life back. There were times that
my belief was sorely challenged, but I always found my way
back. Yes, it was hard. Anything truly meaningful is hard.

If you believe wholeheartedly in yourself, you can achieve
your goals and dreams in any realm. Many people give up
too soon. They lose hope. They fear change or failure. But
our reaction to any challenge dictates the outcome. We
are in charge and must let go of doubt and fear. We must
assume responsibility for this gift of life and cherish it.

I wrote *Say Yes to Life* to inspire readers to find that inner
strength—no matter what challenges they face. We don't
know how strong we are until we have to be.

You may wonder why I chose to donate a portion of book proceeds to St. Jude Children's Research Hospital. I am beyond grateful that I never had to see my own three children suffer the torturous treatments that are sometimes necessary to save lives. I have always adored all children, and I treasure my three gems. I am honored and grateful to be called their Mom, Mumsie, and Mami.

I hope this small token of gratitude contributes to finding cures, and that someone's special angel can be given the chance to "say yes to life" and soar.

Thank you for reading, and remember, we live only once. Make your life wonderful. Learn, embrace, and say yes!

Cheers!

Ilse

1

Passion is the bridge that takes you from pain to change.

—Frida Kahlo

I awoke in an unfamiliar room, on a strange bed, amid tubes and wires and beeping machines. Beneath halos of golden light, my children's faces came into soft focus, portraits of shock and sorrow. As I tumbled back down into the darkness, I heard an angel whisper in my ear, "I love you, Mumsie."

On May 22, 2015, I learned I had stage four oral cancer. One month later, I underwent a three-quarter glossectomy and a tracheotomy. The ten-hour surgery involved cutting out most of my tongue and replacing it with a new tongue made from the tissue of my forearm. Surgeons removed my infected lymph nodes via an incision in my neck.

For seven days after the surgery, I lay in the ICU, completely immobilized and wracked with searing pain. Unable to speak or swallow, I hovered between morphine dreams and a harsh new reality. I had arrived in a place where only the strong-willed survive.

The surgery marked the beginning of a year-long battle for my life. I could not have predicted oral cancer would strike me. But cancer does not discriminate. When it chose me, I came prepared to fight and win.

2

Happiness is a choice, not a result. Nothing will make you happy until you choose to be happy. No person will make you happy unless you decide to be happy. Your happiness will not come to you. It can only come from you.

—Ralph Marston

I have been a citizen of the world since the day I was born in Caracas, Venezuela. By the time I turned five, I spoke four languages. When cancer stole my tongue, I spoke none at all.

Growing up, I heard a variety of languages at home. My parents spoke fluent Spanish, English, German, and Latvian and understood French well enough to get by. My mother conversed with her parents in Russian. My first language was Spanish, and I soon learned Latvian from my grandparents, who lived close by. I attended a

German-speaking kindergarten, and before the age of five, I added English to my repertoire.

My maternal grandfather spoke some Japanese. He gave me an ear for those strange, alien sounds as he bounced me on his lap and talked to me about exotic, faraway places few knew anything about at my age. At my house, a conversation might begin in one language and end in another. We were raised with a sensitivity to the varieties of experience and expression the world offers.

When we moved to the United States, my teachers admired my facility with languages. In seventh grade, an article in the school newspaper made mention of my multilingualism as if it were an amazing accomplishment. How strange, I thought. I exercised no control over this or any of my other perceived talents. While I attended a normal American school, I spent Friday evenings perfecting my Latvian and Saturdays attending a German school. I also competed in figure skating, took tennis lessons, and made time to do homework and attend to any other pursuits my mother assigned.

As a teen, I had no time to date. My schedule was entirely taken up with achieving the perfection my parents expected. Until cancer struck, I lived my life consciously or subconsciously submitting to my parents' vision of me. And then, with the cut of a knife, that carefully sculpted persona ceased to exist. Cancer forced me to find myself beneath the layers of my parents' expectations. Thank God.

M y parents met in Germany, where they both attended university. They were highly educated and placed great value on academics and culture. These were values their parents instilled in them, and they passed them on to their own children.

My mother studied medicine, though she did not pursue this career after marriage. Instead, my dad's goals and dreams became her focus. At the time, this was the norm. Women were expected to support their husbands' careers rather than pursue their own. Despite three miscarriages, my mother had five children.

My mother's first child, Aina, was our half-sister, a troubled child who caused us all a lot of grief. She lived with my maternal grandparents, but she visited us frequently. Aina envied me, and whenever she came to stay with us, she made my life a living hell. My instinct told me there was something wrong with Aina and her place—or non-place—in the family, and I steered clear of her as much as possible.

Aina's emotional issues affected us all, and the conflicts and chaos continued into our adulthood. Her origins were mysterious, and our mother shared no details about her first marriage. She simply refused to talk about Aina's father.

My mother ignored the problems between Aina and the rest of us. She never stepped in to help us resolve our conflicts. My father tried to run interference, but eventually he gave up. In later years, I paid dearly for his turbulent relationship with my half-sister. He had no intention of tolerating her brand of behavior in his own children and went overboard to maintain control over us.

I tried to make peace with Aina to no avail. She was extremely bright, but she was a wild child whose dramas intensified as she got older. Once I had my children, I had no energy for her chaos in my life. I had to let her go. Aina died at age fifty, and, sadly, we never resolved our differences. Because of Aina, I learned ways to deal with crazy at a very early age.

Aina was not the only mystery in my mother's life. She was a woman of many secrets, and she built an impenetrable wall between herself and others, even her family. Her inability or unwillingness to deal with the problems caused by her troubled first child exemplifies how out of touch she was with her emotions.

Beautiful and distant, my mother placed great value on appearances. She was always impeccably dressed, even early in the morning. To her, a sense of style and excellent manners were paramount. To prepare me to ascend to her ideal of womanhood, I attended classes on manners, etiquette, dance, the right sports, and languages. My schedule left little time to be a child or do anything I thought was fun. At the time, I thought this was normal. It wasn't until my teen years that I began to compare myself with my peers and see that all this training was highly unusual.

My mother's guarded nature prevented her from discussing feelings. She rarely told me she loved me, though I knew she did. She preferred to brush difficult situations under the carpet, and she expected us to do the same. When bad things happened, you bucked up and moved on. When my father died, for instance, leaving her a young widow with four children to raise on her own, she betrayed no emotion and offered us no consolation. I knew I didn't want to be that kind of a person.

Luckily, I had a second mother, one who knew how to love.

My mother was not a maternal person. For reasons she did not share, she did not want to involve herself in raising her children. I was her first child after Aina, and soon after I was born, she hired Ketty, my nanny, to care for me. Ketty provided the love my mother could not. She was always available emotionally, and she gave me the capacity to love unconditionally.

Ketty was a tall, slim, beautiful woman. Born in Aragon, Spain, she left after the Civil War and a broken love affair and traveled to Caracas, Venezuela, to visit her sister. At her sister's urging, she answered the advertisement my dad had put out for a nanny. The fact that she was European gave her an edge over the other applicants, I'm sure.

She was fun and always loving, and she taught me how to show emotions and care about others. She believed we should love without hiding it, we should cry when we were hurt, and laugh when we were happy. If not for her, I might have grown up to be an emotionally unavailable person like my mother, with no choice but to repeat the cycle of dysfunction.

My mom barely tolerated Ketty. One incident taught me I could not allow my mom to see how much I loved my nanny. I was three years old and playing dress-up with a friend in the garden. Ketty dragged out our costumes, many of which were discarded items from my mother's closet, and I put one of the dresses on.

"Who are you supposed to be?" my friend asked me. I'm sure she expected me to say I was a princess or a character from a fairy tale.

"Quiteria Olivan Samper," I said.

"Who is that?" my friend asked.

Quiteria Olivan Samper was Ketty's full name, but I didn't say that. Instead, I replied, "That's my mom."

I had no idea my mother was listening from an upstairs terrace, but even if I had known, I would not have thought anything was wrong with referring to Ketty as my mom.

Later that afternoon, my mother fired Ketty.

The loss left me fearful and uncertain about who, if anyone, would take care of me and love me. Her absence left me inconsolable. As the weeks wore on, my grief intensified, and I developed a fever. Finally, my parents checked me into a hospital, where I was diagnosed with a virulent kidney infection.

My father understood that my illness had to do with my heartache over losing Ketty. Ever my champion, and over my mother's objections, he rehired Ketty while I was in the hospital. I don't know what happened between my parents, but I know Dad was very displeased with my mother. In rehiring Ketty he went against her wishes. At the time, I did not understand why my mother was so angry with Ketty, but after the incident, I knew better than to show my real emotions around her.

With Ketty, I felt free to be a child, secure in the knowledge that she would not judge me or abandon me. She transformed normal outings into big adventures. Mundane errands, like selecting fruits at the marketplace, turned into delightful, magical experiences. Ketty enriched my world in countless ways. She was always singing and making up wonderful stories about enchanted princesses or introducing me to ancient fairy tales. Even mealtimes were fun, unlike the rigid and formal dinners my mother presided over. When I got older, she taught me how to handle myself around the young men who were beginning to show an interest.

When I was seventeen, Ketty returned to Spain. Diagnosed with terminal brain cancer, with little time left, she wanted to die in her homeland. I was devastated. Her last months were torturous, and I have always regretted not being by her side during those difficult days. But I was just beginning my freshman year of college, and postponing was not an option. The news of her death crushed me. Ketty had always been with me. I didn't see how I would get through life without my "mom" to confide in.

The one-year contract Ketty and my father signed extended to seventeen. In those years, she taught me how to make my way in life as a loving, compassionate human being. Thank God my dad understood my mother's limitations and how much I needed Ketty in my life.

My dad was a maverick, a self-made man. He did well in his own business, and later, as a top executive with the largest pharmaceutical company in the world at the time. In many ways, including emotionally, I felt protected by him. His career took us all over the world, and no matter where we landed, he always made sure we were well taken care of. He offered us a life of adventure and privilege. We had our differences, but we remained close until the end of his life.

Our family lived in Venezuela until 1958. With the overthrow of the country's dictator, Marcus Perez Jimenez, my dad decided life had become too uncertain. He and my mother set out to find a new home for us. For the next year, they traveled the world looking for a place to restart my dad's career. Ketty stayed with my one-year-old brother and me in New York City. After several months, my parents returned with big news: we would have a little brother or sister. Shortly after their return, we celebrated Christmas. Days later, on my mother's birthday, a baby boy joined our family.

Soon after the birth of my brother, we moved back to Caracas, the site of my fondest childhood memories. I attended grade school in the mornings, and our family always had lunch together at home. We spent weekends at a house on the beach, and if my mother decided to stay, I drove to school with my dad early Monday morning. I loved my life in Caracas and the closeness it enabled with my dad, but when I was ten years old, our time there had to come to an end. We moved permanently to the United States, and he gradually became less of a presence in my life.

We settled in New Jersey. I found it difficult to adapt to the American lifestyle and felt like an outsider among my friends at school. My mom ran a European household. We did not have sliced Wonder bread and peanut butter and jelly or tuna fish and mayonnaise to slather on it. Instead, our kitchen was stocked with tongue, octopus, herring, and countless other exotic items. My typical snack was chocolate and freshly baked bread, maybe a baguette with cheese, a pierogi, plain yogurt with fresh fruit, or a variety of nuts and dried fruits.

Wine at meals was a given. We never had milk, iced tea, or soda. At snack time, my mother often served me a cup of delicious coffee with milk. I say "delicious" because my mother's coffee was not the American watered-down junk that passed for coffee in those days. From her, I learned what real coffee should taste like at an early age.

There wasn't a bag of chips in sight at our house. I had to leave a shopping list of American snacks and change the dinner menus when my school friends came to visit. Our normal fare would have shocked them, and they would never have come back. Though my additions to the grocery list were not denied, I had to listen to my mother's lectures about the unhealthy uncivilized American diet.

We lived very well, and my upbringing had its pluses, such as journeys to luxurious resorts in faraway places. But affluence came with a hefty price tag. The stifling, protective atmosphere I was raised in skewed my attitude toward money. As a child, I was not taught the cost of anything. I never had an allowance. Everything was always provided.

When I moved into an apartment in my last year of college, I informed my dad's secretary, and she filled out the necessary paperwork. My dad paid the rent directly to the landlord. I had nothing to do with it, and I felt it was a huge disservice.

I tried to understand why my dad, who fostered my independence by giving me many opportunities to be a formidable woman, never allowed me to take responsibility for my own finances. I studied economics and worked in various accounting and finance internships, but Dad never discussed money with me. I always thought that this handicapped me. I would have preferred to pay my own bills rather than having them paid by his secretary.

With his death, I ventured into the world like a babe in the woods. My entire family shared the same disadvantage, including my mom. Dad had provided everything for us and shared nothing about his many holdings. He did not prepare us like he should have, and the result was chaotic and scary.

Upon graduation from high school, my dad and I locked horns. He wanted me to attend Vassar or Smith, and I stubbornly resisted, insisting instead on the University of Pennsylvania, which was the first Ivy League school to admit women. I knew Penn would challenge me academically. I planned a concentration in Latin American Studies for one of my majors. I had always loved that part of the world. My best memories were set in Venezuela. In addition to Latin American Studies, I planned to pursue a second major in International Relations, another one of my great passions. I was ambitious, and I set high goals for myself. Dad's vision of my future, however, didn't match my own.

I knew I would grow emotionally and socially at Penn. I had seen what happened to the girls who attended Smith and Vassar. Many of them dropped out after a couple of years because they had accomplished the main aim of attending these schools: they got married to young Ivy League men headed for big careers and the country club. I knew that wasn't for me, and I told my dad so.

My dad's agenda for me involved avoiding the pitfalls he had encountered with Aina. She had really gone off the rails in college, and Dad wanted to see me safely tucked away in one of the great women's colleges. In fact, he insisted. I defied him. "I will go to the University of Pennsylvania whether or not you pay for it," I said. "I will find a way."

He finally relented, and just as I had hoped, I flourished at Penn. However, all the foreign countries I had visited were like my own backyard compared to the strange new world I encountered. Nevertheless, I found kindred spirits in some of the women I met at school. Like me, they had dreams aside from marriage. We held nothing against marriage. It just wasn't a goal or desire. I wanted a meaningful life beyond marriage and family. To me that meant living in the real world, traveling, exploring, working, and expanding my life beyond the protective bubble my parents had created.

I had chosen the right school, but I struggled to adjust. In addition to practical matters of daily life, like paying bills and balancing a checkbook, I was not emotionally prepared. I knew, however, that I could not confide in my parents. I could not let them know how tough it was to navigate one of the largest universities in the country. My dad would have removed me immediately and sent me off to one of the smaller women's colleges.

If my dad had known my true situation, I would have lost what little control of my life I had gained. Once again I would have lived under his tight supervision. Consequently, I made the transition from a protected family life to the real world on my own. I had to adjust to a coed dorm with coed bathrooms, recreational drugs, binge drinking, promiscuity, and much more. I knew my living arrangement unnerved my dad. He was a worldly man. He knew perfectly well what close living quarters would lead to.

"Is that marijuana I smell in the hallway?" he asked when he visited.

I professed ignorance.

Looking inside the bathrooms, he raised his eyebrows. "Do men shower in the stall next to you?"

I dodged that landmine too, but he wasn't fooled.

Seeing how I lived, he visited often. His office was only two-and-a-half hours away. However, no amount of hovering gave him insight into how uncomfortable I felt living in those dorms on that sprawling campus. He could not have helped me learn the ropes. It was not easy at first, but I was able to do it, and eventually, I blended in.

In my first semester at Penn, my roommate contracted a sexually transmitted disease, got pregnant, had an abortion, attempted suicide, and dropped out—all within three months. My roommate had made stupid choices, but I pitied her. Looking back, I am surprised I didn't see my half-sister in this girl. By then I already knew what crazy looked like, and deep down, I knew I should steer clear of her. But that knowledge was still too covered up by layers of longing for connection, for friendship, for belonging.

Naively, I offered advice when she asked. I could not believe she had made such a mess of her life. She was a bright girl, at Penn on a full scholarship, but obviously, she had very little common sense. Her out-of-control behavior frightened me, and when she attempted suicide, I finally saw she had serious emotional problems. Not knowing how to handle the situation, I went numb.

She dropped out of school, and I decided to go home for the weekend. I needed my protective bubble. I had done my best to support her, but I couldn't prevent the chaos she created. That was my initiation into real life. It gave me pause. Perhaps I should have listened to my dad and gone to Smith. But I was no quitter. My misgivings about Penn didn't last long. On Sunday night, I returned to school, and my parents never knew what I had gone through.

Of course, I couldn't tell my parents about my roommate's catastrophic mistakes. My dad's alarm bells would have gone off with echoes of Aina ringing in his ears, and I would have been safely tucked away inside his protective shield forever. I did, however, tell my parents that my roommate had dropped out of school. When I returned from the holidays for my second semester, I had the same room and no roommate. I suspected my dad had intervened on my behalf, but we never talked about it. My months of living like every other freshman coed came to an end. Within the confines of Penn, my dad managed to recreate the shielded environment I had lived in all my life.

Other students struggled to make ends meet while I had a private room and everything I could want. When Dad came to visit, he arrived in a limo with a driver. I always asked to meet him down the street and tried to plan outings away from campus to avoid the issue. Despite my efforts to gain some independence, my dad's control over my life was suffocating me.

I had always pushed back against his will to control me. He had raised me to be strong and independent, but when the time came to let me fly, he could not allow me to become that woman. I decided I would finish college as quickly as possible, get a job, and be done with my dad's stifling attention to every detail of my life. I knew I would have to fight every inch of the way to realize my own dreams. Beyond college, my dad expected to have a say in my career and whom I would marry. He wanted to be sure that my future husband would provide the kind of life he had in mind for me. I wanted only to begin my real life, the one I made on my own.

I spent the summer between my freshman and sophomore years in Germany. Unbeknownst to me, my dad had arranged an internship at one of his offices in Frankfurt. I had no say in the matter. When I went home after my final exams, my dad told me I would be leaving the following week. All I could do was pack my bags and go. There was no use in objecting.

As it turned out, it was a spectacular summer. I stayed with a girlfriend for over three months. My dad purchased a car for me, and on weekends, I set out on my own, exploring Germany, Switzerland, Austria, and Spain.

I developed two distinct personas: the carefree one who drove around Europe having a blast, and the young woman who appeared perfect in my dad's eyes when he came to check on me. I went to great lengths to keep my identity a secret at work. I knew if my co-workers found out who my dad was, they would be guarded around me, and I would not have any friends.

I enjoyed going to have beers after work and getting to know these lovely people who happened to work for my dad. I even told my dad that I wanted to hide my true identity, explaining that I just wanted to be one of the gang. He went along with this for six weeks. Then he arrived and did the unthinkable. He came to see me in my office and insisted we do lunch. His visit was a surprise not only to me, but to my boss and the entire department.

My work environment changed almost overnight. My boss gave me fewer responsibilities, and he praised me for every little task I accomplished. The peers I had been socializing with pulled away. No doubt they were intimidated by the boss's daughter. My dad had blown my cover.

When I wasn't traveling, I was attending social engagements my dad had set up. He made sure I was invited to all the right dances, dinners, and outings in the countryside. I met the son of some family friends at one of these parties. I'm sure my dad orchestrated the whole thing. The man was eight years my senior. I must admit, he was quite nice, perfect in many ways, except one: he was not my choice.

Upon my return to the United States, I met a man I almost married. My dad could not stand him, and that just made him more attractive to me. Deep down I knew he was not the right guy for me, but I had come to realize that in order to get away from my dad, I would need a man to protect me, and he seemed better than the German, who continued to court me relentlessly.

I had grown into a strong, intelligent, beautiful adult, just the kind of woman my dad admired. And yet, these qualities, along with my blossoming sexuality, caused him severe angst. The fact that I was also his favorite child only added to his aggravation when I challenged him. We had many of our legendary fights during this time. He was accustomed to people acquiescing to his wishes, and when I didn't, all hell broke loose. When I knew I was right, I did not budge. He could threaten all he wanted, and I ignored him. Some of our biggest showdowns concerned my refusal to marry the German fellow. Dad finally relented, only because he feared what I might do in defiance of his wishes. He had met his match—a strong-willed woman, the reflection of himself.

My dad and I called a truce. I had proven I would stand up to him, and he knew I would not back down. By the time I graduated from college, we made peace, and I felt in possession of my life at last. My own achievements and missteps promised to shape me. I envisioned myself growing into the woman I was meant to be, not my dad's ideal or my mother's vision of the perfect Ilse.

My newfound freedom enabled me to love my dad more than I ever could when he tried to control me. And then, in the blink of an eye, I lost him. My dad died suddenly, and my world came crashing down.

It took a lot of courage, but I decided I would deliver my dad's eulogy. Looking out over the large crowd, the faces of our friends and family swam together into a murky, sorrow-filled sea. If only I could awaken from this nightmare, I thought, I would have my dad back. But as I recited the words I had written to honor him, I knew I really had lost my father. I would never again see the man who had, in his own way, protected me. In the midst of my deepest grief, I felt gratitude for the peace we made in his last year. After two decades of conflict, he had finally set me free.

I couldn't bear to take part in the cheery gathering after my dad's funeral. Frank Sinatra's "My Way" played in the background, and I wanted to run away, get as far as I could from the song I had heard him play so often on his stereo. Hearing Charles Aznavour had the same effect. The romantic melodies sent me into inconsolable fits of weeping. The music brought up memories of my brilliant father, who lived life in Technicolor, enjoying every moment.

All his life, my dad maintained the high values his parents instilled in him. He held his mother and father as well as his own family, sacred and close. Being the eldest son, he had always taken care of everyone. After he died, we found out how many people outside our family he had sent through college. He bought buses for churches to transport the elderly to events and Sunday services. He lent money to people so they could purchase homes, and he didn't bother to keep a list. He never said a word to us about all the gifts and loans. The recipients of his generosity came to inform us after the funeral, and I was deeply moved. Out of gratitude for his life and his success, he had given back.

At the funeral reception, people ate and drank as if this cataclysmic event hadn't happened, as if we would all go on as we always had, celebrating our good fortunes, living the good life. These nightmarish scenes of feasting went on for days, and I couldn't bear to participate. Even now, when I hear Charles Aznavour, I get a lump in my throat.

I had struggled against my dad's overbearing presence in my life for years, and then, without warning, he vanished. Though he had been my strongest opponent, he had also been my staunchest protector. With his death, the powerful sense of self I earned in our battles retreated and lodged deep down inside, safe from the outside world. My true self slumbered like Sleeping Beauty for more than thirty years, until oral cancer awoke me with its bitter kiss.

My dad was buried in May, one day before my twenty-second birthday. The month had always been a happy time, when we celebrated my dad's birthday and mine. But after Dad's death, I dreaded its arrival. I tried to ignore my birthday for years afterward. Was it synchronicity that I filed for divorce on this date? That I was diagnosed with cancer on the very same date? Oral cancer, no less? Most likely not. If there's one thing I have learned in my spiritual quest, it is that there are no coincidences in life.

I met the man I married in Guatemala, where I was doing coursework for a master's degree and he was taking some classes. I planned to enter the foreign service after graduate school. However, our relationship set me on the first of several major detours in my life.

In many ways, we were a good match. We had common interests in languages, travel, and culture. We both came from emotionally unavailable families, but, while I had the seemingly perfect family, he was a child of divorce. He had basically raised himself and kept to himself. He and his siblings did not get along. No one helped him with his lessons. He taught himself. And the family didn't bother with celebrating holidays. I thought he and I could strike a good bargain: he and I would create the family he longed for and together we would reach for our many dreams. This, I thought, could be a marriage that could last a lifetime.

Ours was a long-distance relationship right up to the day we married. I was working in New York, and he was in Mexico. We spent long weekends and vacations together, but that didn't afford us much opportunity to get to know each other. We were always on holiday when we were together, never living our ordinary lives. Consequently, I didn't see any of the warning signs of the real damage his family inflicted on him. If I had, I would have seen that, like me, he had been hurt, only I had Ketty and the protective shield she created for me. He, on the other hand, had no protection at all. I learned a very expensive lesson: I could not fix these emotional wounds he bore, and he was not willing to address them. But that's hindsight. At the time, I saw only what I wanted to see.

If I had my way, we would have eloped. I could not bear the thought of anyone but my dad walking me down the aisle and giving me away. A brother or an uncle could have substituted, but that would have been meaningless. The only person I could have allowed that honor was my father.

His mother found out we were considering eloping, and she informed my mother. Both of them wanted an elegant wedding, and neither was going to back down. I gave in, but, ever my father's hardheaded daughter, I refused to take part in the preparations. The mothers planned the entire extravaganza, which took place one month after they found out about our plans to elope. I acquiesced to one dress fitting and showed up at the ceremony. And no one took my father's place. I walked down the aisle alone and gave myself away.

Two weeks after our wedding, in August 1983, we moved to Dallas. We had already bought a house in Highland Park, and my husband enrolled in the law school at Southern Methodist University. Early-1980s Dallas, with its blue laws and Southern ways, gave me quite a shock after living in New York City. I wondered how long we would have to live in such a place. Over time, I came to overlook the downsides and appreciate all the positive things about Dallas. The city became home, and thirty-four years later, I still love living here.

From the beginning of our marriage, I gave a lot of thought to how I would raise my children. I had always loved children, and thanks to Ketty, some of my happiest memories were of my early years. I knew, though, that I would not repeat my parents' mistakes. I did not want my husband to control me or our children, and no nanny would take over raising them. Perhaps most important, in my new family, talking about emotions would be highly encouraged. I decided that my children would always be invited to discuss their issues with me or their dad. My children were not going to be too frightened to speak up. They would not have to bottle up their emotions. I would always tell them I loved them, and I would teach them that love is not a form of weakness. On the contrary, it is a sign of strength.

M y son, Paul, was born in the fall of 1985, six months before his dad's graduation from law school. We had thought of moving from Highland Park, but once Paul arrived, we found it was a *Leave It to Beaver* paradise for raising a family.

Since church was such an integral part of the Dallas lifestyle, we opted to join the Presbyterian Church. You would have thought we would give more weight to such an important decision, but it was more like joining a country club. My children attended Sunday school and received the proper religious training, even though we did not practice religion at home. Eventually my children could decide if organized religion was for them, I thought, just as my parents had left that decision up to me.

The twins, Aina and Andie, were born four years after Paul. The kids attended elementary school in Highland Park, which I thought was fine, except for the general attitude toward Spanish speakers. Highland Park is not a diverse community. There's a reason it's called "The Bubble." The closest contact most people have with Hispanics is with their housekeepers, nannies, and gardeners. My children's father is Mexican, and I wanted to ensure that my children would not suffer the indignities often faced by minorities in insular Anglo communities. As soon as they entered kindergarten, I began volunteering, teaching Spanish to the kids at school and introducing them to Mexican culture.

Once the kids reached adolescence, we had many roller coaster rides involving the typical teenage issues. In our household that meant huge emotional explosions. My husband could not understand that this was normal, that we were humans and not unfeeling objects. At this point, it became harder and harder to keep the family together. The foundation of our marriage and our family definitely began to shake.

While life at home was becoming more and more intense, school life seemed to me to be less and less supportive of growing young adults. Plus, I wanted my kids to get a broader worldview, as I had. When my kids reached highschool age, I noted a misplaced emphasis on the outer shell of a person—makeup, clothes, et cetera—in Highland Park. It was all about football and cheerleading. I wanted them to learn languages, play sports, and delve into world cultures and the arts. Though I knew I would miss them terribly, I decided to send them to boarding schools in the East.

Boarding school offered many advantages over the local schools, but there were plenty of pitfalls for adolescents. At that critical age, when they were gaining their identity, they needed guidance emotionally, and that was certainly not part of the curriculum. I stayed intimately involved in their lives, offering guidance and support, even though they were thousands of miles away. I traveled often to see them in order to remain a major presence.

My husband's work took him all over the world, and the children and I often traveled with him. Just like my father, my husband provided a comfortable life for us. And just as I did as a child in my father's house, I came to feel increasingly empty in the home I made with my husband. Life had led me to the country club, after all. I had always known this was not what I wanted, and yet, here I was.

Gradually, I began to look for ways to make my life more fulfilling. It wasn't that I had emotional problems that anyone would see on the outside. I had buried that vulnerable real self along with my dad, and I appeared to be perfect, just as my parents had trained me to be. I did not have problems with alcohol or drugs, and I didn't suffer from mental illness. But I did suffer from emotional dis-ease. From deep down, my self was calling out to me. I knew I wanted more out of life.

While my husband conducted business in foreign countries, I explored. In the year 2000, we traveled in Asia for three months with our children. We arrived in Siem Reap, Cambodia, right after the country opened for tourism. I visited Angkor Wat, the largest temple complex in the world. The experience focused my search for spirituality and started my clock ticking faster to resolve my inner issues.

On our private tour of Ankor Wat, the guide shared his life story with us. He was a child during the Pol Pot regime when the Khmer Rouge terrorized the country for four long years. He had witnessed the killing fields and watched as his parents and four of his eight siblings were lined up and shot to death.

I was horrified. "You must be so happy that Pol Pot is dead."

He shook his head. "I let go of that anger a long time ago," he said. "I knew if I held on to it, it would destroy me and everyone I loved."

His wisdom impressed me, and I asked him about his life after Pol Pot.

"I have my own thriving business, a wonderful wife, and three children," he said.

"Are you religious?"

"I am a Buddhist."

I observed how much respect he and other Cambodians seemed to have for their families. Their children did not appear to be extensions of their parents. Unlike many parents in the West, Cambodians displayed great respect for their children.

I told my husband the guide's story as well as what I had observed. "Don't you see?" I said. "We didn't learn how to parent like this because our parents didn't respect us. But we can change. We can honor our children's dreams and help them achieve their goals, not our goals for them."

He looked at me as if I had spoken in a foreign tongue. I knew then that my husband saw my children and me as possessions, bought and paid for. He had no interest in our children's dreams or mine. In that moment, I understood that only I would practice this respectful approach to parenting our children. Their father would likely never partner with me in this, and that had to be okay. I had to let go of expectations.

In Cambodia, I began my journey toward emotional healing and spiritual growth. "Hate eats you up," and "Live in the present," were the words that echoed in my mind from that trip. The Cambodians showed me the peace I might find if I reclaimed my self, a self that had become buried deeper and deeper with every loss, barricaded behind rules I learned from my family, instructions to deny feelings and armor against the real me.

I had been seeing therapists off and on all my adult life. There must be more healing modalities than shrinks and pharmaceuticals, I thought. I began venturing into alternative medicine, acupuncture, and past-life regression for relief from the emotional pain of my difficult marriage.

My spiritual explorations provided unexpected benefits. As my sense of self strengthened, so did my creativity. I became an accomplished cook. I wrote. And I began decorating the house with greater self-confidence. I had taken numerous art classes as a child, and I felt drawn to returning to that pursuit.

During a vacation in Venice, my son told his sisters about his visit to the Peggy Guggenheim Collection on the Grand Canal. The twins wanted to go, and I thought it would be wonderful, but I stayed behind with my husband. He had no interest in modern art, which he thought was just a lot of scribble scrabble. The twins loved it, and to my joy, returned very happy. I knew I was on the right track, letting them form and develop, not stifling their growth and controlling them.

How can you develop into an interesting person if you do not know what you like or dislike? We are all distinct beings with different goals and dreams. The child may exhibit similar traits as the parents, but can never be exactly like the parent. Everyone has to find their own path in life. It didn't occur to me at the time that I was denying myself the opportunity for the growth I was giving to my children.

That came later. First, I had to begin exploring my deeper self.

I began working with a variety of spiritual teachers. The more I searched, the more clarity evolved. With great regret, I realized that I had repeated some of the negative patterns of my childhood, though I had fervently wished to escape them. I had married someone like my mother, who was emotionally unavailable and could not share his feelings. History also repeated itself in another way. I followed my husband around the world just like my mother followed my dad when I was a child. I had to break these negative patterns. To do so, I set about learning all I could about spirituality. I was determined to find any and all tools available to me for emotional healing.

I could never discuss what I was exploring with my husband, as he truly did not want to understand. He was perfectly at peace with our life. The few times I had decided to talk to him about it, he ignored me. He felt my confrontations created the issues. He blamed every argument on me, believing if I did not question our relationship, all would be fine. I finally accepted that it would be best not to question his behavior. Rather, I would search for knowledge that would free me and give me happiness. I tried to make the most out of the life we had as a family. In his presence, when sad things happened, I did as my mother had taught me. I simply bucked up and kept going. But around my children, I modeled different behavior. I wanted to be sure they would not repeat the emotional unavailability that my husband and I grew up with.

Seeing the damage being done to my children hurt me deeply. I adored them and devoted myself to being a wonderful mom. I taught them that emotions are normal, instinctual responses to life experiences. They are biochemical reactions in your body that result in laughter, tears, trembling, weakness in the knees, and countless other physical manifestations. I recalled my mother's complete absence of tears or any other signs of emotion when my father died, and I was determined not to repeat her abnormal behavior. I modeled healthy behavior around emotions and took great pains to explain how important it is to "wear your heart on your sleeve."

I taught my children the difference between emotions and feelings, and that suppressing either is not healthy. I explained that feelings are our normal reactions to emotions. Our minds associate the physical state that produces tears, for instance, with the feeling of sadness. I knew how much damage had been done by my mother especially, and I was determined not to repeat the pattern.

From an early age, my children knew they could tell me anything, good or bad. It took more than determination to break the bad habits I learned from my parents. I had to learn a whole new way to approach life. I had to develop my own modus operandi. Over time, my seeking and education paid off. The bond I have with my children is unbreakable.

Unfortunately, my husband had no interest in letting go of the negative effects of his childhood. He was on his own path, refusing to confront himself and his demons. Though we had many adventures and lots of interesting travels together, our conflicts grew. I was not outgrowing him because of interests or intelligence, but because he would not deal with his issues.

Time and again, he refused to explore himself, our relationship, and our problems as a family. I do believe marriage is for better or worse, and I would not have left if he had been willing to address his issues. But he chose to ignore them and act like everything was perfectly fine.

I realized, too, that his problems were beyond my power to solve. I could not be with someone who did not want to help himself, someone who chose to pull others down with him. His issues had become ours. It was like a disease in a healthy tree. No matter how much the tree is watered and receives sunlight, the disease stunts its growth and withers the leaves. We were all affected, and I knew our life together would never change. I had tried to make my broken marriage work, but finally, I had to face the fact that it could not be fixed. The kindest thing I could do for myself and our children was show them what an emotionally healthy life looks like.

We had come to the end of our road, and yet, I could not accept that. Divorce was out of the question in my family. In fact, the word *divorce* was like the word cancer, a forbidden term. I didn't even know what the word meant until I was eight or nine years old. We were expected to be perfect in all areas of life, including marriage. So, for nearly three decades, I resisted defeat.

I am a firm believer that you cannot tell your children, "Do as I say, not as I do." We lead through example. Though I had been conditioned to resist the idea of divorce, I knew that for my sake and my children's sake, I could not get to where I needed to be in life walking my husband's path. I had to go on alone. I knew that walking away from the marriage would give me the peace I sought.

Thirty years after I met him and twenty-six years into the marriage, I filed for a divorce.

The divorce, like most divorces, was very difficult. Luckily, we did not have custody issues. Paul was twenty-four, and the twins were twenty. I could not imagine co-parenting after such a vicious procedure. For our children's sake, I wished we had agreed at the time of our marriage we would work on a divorce amicably if it happened and not allow legalities to feed the fire. All it takes is a simple agreement with your husband and best friend to respect each other and the family that once existed. No matter what age the children are, when you go through the end of a marriage, they suffer. Hindsight is always perfect. Unfortunately, there are no redos.

Although the attraction between us was great, I realized when I left the marriage that it had been doomed from the start. He was an emotionally unavailable person, and I was the opposite—I had had enough experience with such in my childhood and had put it behind me. He was not someone I should have attracted into my life. He had not soared past his childhood, but I had, and this affected our relationship irreparably.

Our marriage ended before we could take up residence in a home designed by an architect to suit my every desire. Situated on a double lot in the heart of Dallas, with six bedrooms and a pool, it represented everything I had ever wanted. By the time construction began on the new house, the divorce was final. The children were all grown and living in New York or overseas. For the first time in nearly thirty years, I was alone. My perfect house felt like a monstrous, empty prison, not a home with a foundation in family. I knew I could not live in this beautiful place, built to house the illusion of a happy marriage. I had awakened from the dream.

The divorce brought welcome relief, but going out into the world on my own felt strange. Relearning how to date proved to be an awkward experience. Settling into being me posed a challenge. Yet, with introspection I realized I had always been on my own. It was quite lonely, even with all my activities and friends in Dallas, and it didn't take long to decide I had to make use of the time I had on my hands. My life needed to move on from the pause mode that accompanied the long and difficult untangling. In order to move forward with my life, I had to leave Dallas.

The market had just gone through a crash, so selling the house wasn't an option. I leased it instead, and within two weeks, I packed and stored furnishings that filled my six-thousand-square-foot home. That alone was a freeing experience. Once I decided to make big changes in life, they came at me with lightning speed. The doors to my past closed swiftly behind me, and I had no choice but to move on.

3

*3 C's of Life: Choices, Chances, and Changes. You must make
a choice to take a chance, or your life will never change.*

—Jacob A. Cowell

My sense of adventure is so ingrained that I cannot imagine navigating life without traveling the world. Naturally, when my marriage ended, the obvious response to this upheaval was a trip. Not just any trip, but a journey, an exploration into the unmined possibilities for my future self.

I planned to take lessons in art, pursue spirituality, explore new places and old haunts, and linger over hours-long meals with my friends. Above all, I intended to live on my own terms. I fully expected the year of travel to serve as a healing rite of passage from my old life to my future. In many ways, these dreams for my sojourn came to pass, though, as is true in all adventures, there were many rewards and a few setbacks I had not foreseen.

The journey began in December 2012, when I left Dallas and decamped to Santa Fe, New Mexico, with my twelve-year-old Bichon Frise, Titan, a fourteen-pound curly white bundle of energy and love. We settled into a small furnished adobe on Acequia Madre, right off Canyon Road in the historic district. The house belonged to an artist, and the owner's works cluttered every room in the place. When I first arrived, I found it bothersome, but gradually, I became well acquainted with the artist's life, her works, and her treasures. I studied her work and hoped one day to paint as masterfully. The house had character and charm, and it offered a peaceful refuge. I spent many hours in the courtyard with Titan by my side, painting and just being.

Early every morning, Titan and I set out on a walk down Canyon Road in the brisk winter air. We stopped often to admire works on display in gallery windows and ended at a coffee house, sitting by a fireplace. I sipped my caffè latte while Titan lapped his foamed milk, a special treat for him. A sprint up Canyon Road brought us back home for breakfast.

Later in the morning, I attended yoga, which I enjoyed thoroughly, and art classes, which struck me as too robotic. I followed instruction meticulously, but because it was so strictly guided, my work exhibited none of my personality. Nevertheless, I was relearning how to make art and getting back to an exercise regimen that balanced and invigorated me.

I did not know it then, but subconsciously, I was drawn to Santa Fe for more than the art and the opportunity to spend time with old friends. Santa Fe is well known as a center of physical and spiritual healing, which made it the ideal place to begin the journey into my new life.

I began consulting with a holistic practitioner named Lupita Gurulé dé Martinéz. Lupita is a shaman and a gifted intuitive medium. I met her by chance, but I have learned most things happen for a reason. I had been going to a massage therapist trained in Eastern Medicine. When I complained of stiffness in my neck, she thought it was stress-related and suggested acupuncture. I was familiar with acupuncture from having had it often and believed in its healing abilities.

The stress diagnosis did not surprise me. I had leased my home in Dallas, and within two weeks, cleared out all the furnishings, put them into storage, and found a place to live in Santa Fe. That didn't even take into account the recent divorce and my impending journey. Of course I was stressed.

I returned often to my acupuncturist, and soon the symptoms cleared. From time to time we talked about energy work. "We are all made up of energy," she said.

I agreed, thinking of what I had learned in my physics classes. But she was talking about auras and chakras, and this was something new to me. Fascinated, I asked her where she had learned all this. I longed for the knowledge she had. I wanted to sign up for whatever class would teach me how to fill this void inside me. "Is there not a place where I could learn more about this energy stuff?"

"There are a lot of people here who do this work," she said. She was rather vague and not particularly forthcoming.

I persisted. "Can you give me their names?"

She mentioned Lupita Gurulé dé Martinéz. I called her that afternoon and set up an appointment. Though I am usually quite articulate, I did not really know what I wanted or what this was all about. I just knew I wanted to speak with her and find out what I could learn about energy work.

I shared this with a friend, and she tried to frighten me, telling me this was all a sham and I would just spend a lot of money. After that, I decided not to share this information with anyone. Though I do not consider myself arrogant, I was pretty sure I could figure out if this was what I wanted. I was not physically ill, desperate for a cure. I was intrigued, and having promised myself to go beyond my comfort zone, I pursued this new avenue, not knowing where it would lead.

I had met a shaman once in Oaxaca, Mexico, in a dark hut lit by candles, the air thick with incense. I considered that encounter more of a performance for tourists than a real experience. Though I didn't expect a primitive shack, I was a bit surprised at the space that housed Lupita's Center for Transformation and Intuitive Arts/Pamper the Spirit. I could have been in any one of my psychotherapist's offices. Soothing colors and soft, comfortable chairs invited me into her waiting room. I felt an immediate sense of calm and peace.

She greeted me with a warm smile and said my first name correctly. It's a phonetic name, yet in English it gets butchered. I felt at ease, even more so when our conversation began traveling back and forth between Spanish and English. She had learned many of her healing practices in Peru. In a soothing tone of voice, she talked to me about family karma, past-life regression, energy, and visualization. I felt respected, never pushed or prodded to do something uncomfortable.

I decided to begin with past-life regression. I wasn't sure I believed in reincarnation, but I was open to the possibility. I was very specific that I did not want to ingest anything or take any drugs, and Lupita reassured me the regression would be done through hypnosis. Four days later, I experienced my first session, and with that, my spiritual journey took a new and exciting turn. Little did I know that within two years, my very survival would depend on the knowledge I gained working with Lupita.

Running away from your problems is a race you will never win. This was a quote I had read in a magazine at the tea shop the morning of my first past-life regression with Lupita. I have learned there is no such thing as coincidence. The universe was most likely sending me a very clear message about my upcoming visit. Until recently, I had tried not to face many things, and as a result, I wasn't happy. I was running, not winning.

Titan accompanied me to my first session. He went everywhere with me and always behaved like a gentleman. He met Lupita with his tail wagging, indicating his approval. Seeing that put me even more at ease. With Titan close by, I laid down on a bed in one of Lupita's serene treatment rooms, listening to the sounds of waves and chirping birds.

Lupita tapped me with some kind of an instrument and told me to close my eyes. I drifted off to a different level of consciousness, not sleep. She began counting, and with every number, I fell deeper and deeper into myself. At some point, I arrived in one of my past lives.

I know it sounds very strange, but the experience was very real and profound. Lupita explained later that you keep repeating what you never came to terms with in a former life. Wow! In that first journey into a past life, I discovered that I had been at the mercy of controlling people even back then. Lupita had no idea about my issues with my dad and how I had fought against his control over my life. She wasn't aware of the same problem following me into my marriage. And yet, with her guidance, I had arrived at the greatest stumbling block in my path.

Together, we examined this past life, and the origin of this control issue began to emerge. When I returned to the present, I felt energized and relieved. With this first glimpse, I felt confident I could venture further.

This kind of energetic work cannot be rushed. We can only accept what we are ready for. Earlier in my life, I would not have been open to exploring my past lives, but on that day in Santa Fe, I arrived at an important new phase in my spiritual development.

On subsequent visits with Lupita, I did healing work on an energetic level. She helped me see that certain aspects of my relationships with important people in my life—my half-sister Aina, my mother, my dad, and my husband—had required coping skills that I no longer needed. It was time to let go of them with kindness. Only then could I resurrect the Ilse hiding deep inside. I felt there was so much to learn and so little time, but she urged me not to push it and advised me to let my growth evolve naturally.

As part of my exploration into alternative modalities, I took a class on Thai massage, which combines acupressure, Ayurveda, and yoga postures. In my training, I learned it was started as preventative medicine for the monks. Though I never intended to give anyone aside from my immediate family a massage, I enjoyed learning how to do this rather difficult work.

The class gave me a deeper understanding of the complexities of the human body and piqued my interest in various types of yoga, which I eventually pursued. Though I am a fan of massages, I have always been sensitive to the energy of the person massaging me. This was before I understood energy, but I already knew that I needed to feel comfortable and at peace with the person making this deep connection with me. This quirk of mine hinted at my openness to energies and hastened my progress with Lupita.

In just a few weeks, I had come to rely on Lupita, and she assured me she would not abandon me once I left Santa Fe. She promised we would stay in touch via phone and email. The sessions we had together enabled me to use what I learned on my own, and when that wasn't enough, I could always reconnect with her. As it happened, Lupita and I maintained a crucial and highly beneficial connection for a very long time.

In Santa Fe, I began to paint the canvas of my new life, and just as a formidable artwork develops slowly, this too promised to take time. I felt my work with Lupita had set me on the right track. I was recapturing me, and a sense of peace began to grow in my heart.

In that small house on Acequia Madre, I began simplifying my life. I had always been a clotheshorse. I loved fashion, and, as a highly creative person, I expressed myself partly through the strong sense of style I inherited from my mother. When a couple of my girlfriends came to visit me, they asked if there was a closet big enough for all my wonderful clothes. I pointed to a small closet, which held everything I would travel with for the coming year. It all fit into one small bag for weekends and a medium suitcase for everything else.

I vowed to buy only those items I fell in love with or absolutely needed. The experience of putting all my possessions in storage had horrified me. I couldn't believe how much I had collected over the years, and how unnecessary most of it was. That process liberated me. I believe we are the authors of complications by our own bad choices or deeds. Clearly, life can be quite simple.

My time in Santa Fe marked the beginning of a great adventure involving outer and inner terrains. I deepened my meditation, began exploring energy work, and released a lot of baggage, both physical and emotional. With Lupita's guidance, I learned to visualize, which is the key to manifesting. I had begun to visualize "as if." By acting as if I could, I manifested my goals. As a result, my internal life came into focus. At the same time, my earthbound, physical sojourn began to take shape.

In Santa Fe, I formulated a plan for a true departure from the life I had been living in Dallas for nearly thirty years. I modeled it after the memoir *Eat, Pray, Love*, about the journey Elizabeth Gilbert undertook after the dissolution of her marriage. Only instead of prayer, I intended to throw myself wholeheartedly into my art, which has been a consistent source of deep satisfaction for me all my life.

I could have stayed in Santa Fe or rented a house in San Miguel Allende, a cosmopolitan artists' community in Mexico I had visited often. But travel is something embedded in my DNA. My parents passed on their sense of adventure and adaptability to me. I felt this was the perfect opportunity to relive the good times I experienced with them.

My journey began in earnest in Paris. I filled my days with fabulous French food, making and viewing art, and rediscovering a self-confidence that eluded me for too many years. I visited museums and galleries and wiled away hours with friends at bistros and sidewalk cafés. Paris is a great walking city, and Titan and I spent hours every day wandering through neighborhoods capturing the magic of life in one of the great cities of the world.

As my life changed, so did my art. I had been painting landscapes, but during my stay in Paris, I began working on abstracts. Instead of interpreting the views around me, I began to paint interiors—my interior. On my canvases, some emotions that I had been afraid to reveal emerged from the darkness, where they had languished far too long.

I don't believe my growth as an artist can simply be attributed to Paris, though it is an inspiring city. No, my painting became more personal. My personality shone through as I gathered more confidence. As a result, my art took on a unique, special quality, one that could only be attributed to me.

I have always appeared confident. Yet there is an aura one exudes when one is happy with one's self. In Paris, I began to approach happiness I had not felt in a long time. Little things made me smile. I felt like a child in a candy store, purchasing art supplies, wanting to try all sorts of new techniques. In my abstract art I found I could express myself as I never had in a still life or landscape. This was the gift of Paris and all that came before.

When I was a child, my family spent many summers traveling throughout Europe by car. One of my favorite destinations was Spain, a place I knew well even before we vacationed there. Ketty had made me fall in love with her homeland as a child. She would tell me about the customs, the food, and her family. She taught me how to play the castanets, and I memorized the words to every Spanish Christmas carol. Thanks to Ketty, my heart was always Mediterranean or Latin, though my genetic makeup was purely Northern European. My favorite vacations were spent in S'Agaró at the luxurious Hostal de La Gavina.

Riding the rollercoaster at the Tibidabo amusement park as a young girl, I saw the modernist architecture of Antoni Gaudí far below me and felt energized and enchanted by this beautiful city. Naturally, Barcelona played a starring role in my journey of renewal.

After about a month in Paris, Titan and I traveled to the scene of these happy summer vacations. I leased an apartment across from Citadella Park in the Born district, close to the Hostal de La Gavina where my family always stayed. Though I loved Paris, I never felt at home as much as I did in Barcelona.

I continued with art classes, and my paintings bloomed. In a short time, my art deepened as it took on even more of my personality. The paintings began to express the true self I was discovering.

Only a few months into my journey, my hopes of finding myself were coming to fruition. I experienced a sense of rediscovery, gradually regaining the person I was before marriage and children. I have always loved being a mom, but the time when my children needed my undivided attention had passed. This journey marked the beginning of my independence. I embraced the carefree attitude of the girl I had once been, and the feeling was beautiful.

During this time, I continued communicating with Lupita, sharing with her my achievements and the answers I was finding to some of my innermost questions. Though I was thousands of miles away, my ally in this journey remained at my side.

Life in Barcelona echoed my time in Paris. My days were filled with art classes, food, and friends, whom I often met up with for tapas and drinks. After a late afternoon siesta, I painted until 10:30, when I went out for dinner. These nightly feasts lasted into the early morning hours. This is the typical life in Barcelona, and it suited me perfectly.

In addition to my old friends, I met new ones in a cooking class directed by a top chef who showed us how to plan meals around the foods of the season. After eating the lunch we cooked, we gathered at a nearby café to discuss food, our lives, and politics. I was fortunate to know Spanish. That made it easy to fit in and really get to know people.

My life was filled with all the things I love most: food, cooking, art, conversation, and friendship. An added bonus was the beach, which was a ten-minute walk from my apartment. Titan and I walked there often, enjoying the fresh air and the soul-reaching seascapes.

My daughters and friends visited every couple of months, just to see what I was up to. I have always loved a full house, and I enjoyed sharing my new world and my blossoming artwork. They all could see that I was very happy and that my life was changing for the better. They agreed Barcelona suited me, and there seemed to be no reason to leave any time soon.

I moved to a beautiful apartment in the Gotico District, about five minutes from El Born. The medieval building on a quiet, winding street was quite unusual, and I still count myself fortunate for the opportunity to stay there. It had been completely gutted, and all the modern facilities replaced the ancient rooms.

My daughter Andie and a friend visited for a couple of days to help me celebrate my birthday. I felt like a local, taking them around, showing off my city. By then, I had extended my stay from one month to nearly four, and saw no end in sight.

After seeing Andie and her friend off, I went back upstairs to my bedroom to change clothes. When I touched the closet doors, I felt tremendous heat. Then I opened them, and gold flames burst out and lunged at me. I reared back and slammed the door shut.

Somehow I had the presence of mind to grab my small suitcase and throw in my passport, some cash, and Titan's documents. I raced to the private elevator. Too late. The fire had already spread through the walls, and I could not use it. I backed away to the phone in the living room and called my landlord, the fire department, and my downstairs neighbor.

Titan and I waited for rescue at the window. I held him in my arms and felt his tiny body shivering with fright. My own fear rose with every second we remained trapped in that apartment. At last I heard the siren, but the fire truck didn't appear. Looking down at the narrow winding street, it struck me that the fire truck could not reach us. We were on the fourth floor. I could not save us on my own.

A crowd gathered. All eyes were on Titan and me. My neighbors shouted reassurances. I heard someone yell,

"Here they come!" The firefighters trotted up the street on foot, hauling a trampoline mattress. Everyone made room as they positioned it under my window. From my vantage point, it looked like an impossibly small target to hit.

Gathering all my courage, I threw Titan out the window then leaped out after him. I was terrified, of course, but I had no choice. I had to do it.

The firefighters wrapped Titan and me in a blanket. They told me we had gotten out just in time. As we sat there, my apartment and the one above were completely destroyed. I lost everything in the fire, but I felt the power of my new-found self-confidence. I had acted quickly and decisively. I had overcome the terror of flinging my dog and myself into the unknown, and we had survived intact, shaken, but otherwise unscathed.

The experience left me rattled. I couldn't sleep. Memories of the experience recurred every time I closed my eyes. I feared every small noise might be another fire. I could not remain. Though I cherished my time there, a few days later, after settling my affairs, I left Barcelona and returned to the United States.

My journey did not come to an end in Barcelona. Rather, it deepened. My leap from the flames led me into uncharted territory, where fears had lain dormant my entire life. Not ready to face them, I resisted, and anxiety consumed me. The fire had peeled away layers of protection, and only Lupita could help me navigate the treacherous new course. I set up two sessions with her, and subliminally, she helped me deal with the fire and the emotions it brought up. Thanks to those sessions and some medications, my anxieties subsided. I was able to get past that horrible experience and move on. I started feeling great again. I knew I was stronger; I had changed.

My next stop was San Miguel Allende, high in the mountains of central Mexico. I rented a lovely house inside a compound with scenic views of La Parroquia, the massive, pink Gothic-style church that presides over the center of the city. I know Mexico very well, having spent a lot of time there, so it was quite easy for me to navigate the culture, and with many friends there, I wasn't lonely. Sometimes I visited friends in Mexico City, and though these visits were wonderful, I always loved returning to the serenity of San Miguel, where I heard church bells ringing instead of the roar of city traffic. The beautiful environs offered an ideal setting for my inner explorations.

I continued with yoga classes, meditated, and practiced the visualizations I learned from Lupita. Art remained an important vehicle in my inner journey. I walked to my art classes at Instituto Allende every morning, and with the encouragement of my teachers there, my work took on new dimensions, infused with the intense emotion that surfaced after the fire.

I loved my time in Mexico and could have stayed there for much longer, but I felt the pull of Europe, as if I had left something undone, unexplored. After three months in San Miguel, I returned to Paris, the true home of my heart. Titan stayed with my daughters in New York, and a girlfriend accompanied me on this leg of my journey.

My friend and I explored the unknown places of the city we both love, as well as the nooks and crannies of our longstanding friendship and the many intertwined people in our lives. During that time, we came to understand each other as we never had, and our relationship blossomed. We talked about my soul-searching and shared stories about the loves in our lives, past and present. She critiqued my work, and I respected her opinion. She is an artist too, an incredible jeweler, and thanks to her contacts, we attended a jewelry auction at Christie's.

One long evening, over drinks at The Shangri La Hotel, we spent hours discussing our love lives—what went wrong and what went right. It had been over three years since my marriage had ended, and I had finally allowed a man in my life. But during this trip, I decided to let him go. I had come to two important realizations: I do not want to change anyone, and love shouldn't be complicated. I knew I needed to be true to my self. This, after all, was what I had been trying to achieve. I knew now what I wanted, and most importantly, what I did not want. My travels were doing their work.

I had renewed faith in myself. The self-confidence that had been dormant flourished. The evening at The Shangri La Hotel solidified what I wanted out of life. I had enjoyed love, yet now I knew what I could live with and what would not work. Our conversation led me to a conclusion I had not foreseen, but there it was: I had learned to love myself.

Since leaving Dallas, my art had developed beyond my wildest imagination. The art lessons, the places I visited, and the friends I made—all contributed to my tremendous growth as an artist. Much of my work hangs in the apartment Andie and Aina share. I visit often, and when I look at the paintings, they reveal much about my struggles, the questions I was asking, the answers that came to me.

My favorite painting is about the fire in Barcelona. It is a very large canvas that hangs in a prominent place in Andie and Aina's living room. Slashes of orange, red, a bit of black, and green assault the viewer, daring her to enter the terror of that day. That leap in Barcelona with Titan marked the beginning of many more courageous leaps I took to save my life. Whenever I look at that painting, it moves me. I see that apartment in flames. But now, I no longer experience the fear. I see it as part of my incredible journey.

My last days in Paris were bittersweet. I enjoyed every moment, as I had all that year and a half. Unquestionably, I had grown. Old friendships were renewed, my relationship with myself deepened, and my art gained power and authenticity. I had, indeed, reconnected with the life I once loved, and I felt ready to return to Dallas and an exciting new life on my own.

Like breathing in the scent of snow in the air, I sensed the next phase coming. I didn't know what the future held, but I felt ready for it. Armed with all the good memories of my journey, I knew I could endure whatever might be in store for me.

4

When you face adversity, you need to remind your-self that whatever is trying to defeat you could very well be what God will use to promote you.

—Joel Osteen

I n early spring 2014, I returned to Dallas, tired and glad to be home. I rested on my couch in the house designed to fulfill my every wish in every room. After living in borrowed houses for so long, settling back into my own home should have elicited joy and relief. Instead, a feeling of profound discomfort overtook me. I lay there and gazed at the beautifully furnished room and the sprawling grounds outside my window. An oppressive silence settled on the house, and through it, I heard a message loud and clear: I could not live here anymore.

After all I had experienced and all I had discovered about myself, I could not call this place home. Instead, it was just another object I didn't see a use for. On my journey, I learned that I didn't want to devote my energies to maintaining a residence. I needed time to explore my inner self and to experience my recaptured happiness. The time had come to sell this monstrous house that served a life I no longer embraced.

The place sold almost immediately, which presented a challenge I wasn't quite ready for. I had not found another place to live. I had already closed on the sale of the house when a friend of mine found a high-rise apartment in the center of Dallas. As soon as I walked in, I knew it was perfect for me.

Titan and I settled in happily. I had a view of a walking trail and a park from my balcony and lots of greenery all around. I moved in only the pieces I had collected and cherished. Anything that didn't suit my new life never crossed the threshold. I created a peaceful, elegant setting that reflects who I am, where I have been, and what I call home. It is my sanctuary.

The walls of my serene new space are shades of whites and neutrals. I wanted the art to be the focal point and the source of color in the rooms. Every object reflects a part of my past and myself. Door panels from Europe carved with detailed scenes of medieval knights and ladies hang on my dining room wall. In the living room, a replica of a carved wood trough from a Mexican ranch serves as a coffee table. Keepsakes of my world travels, including Buddhist scrolls from Myanmar, crystals, Egyptian bracelets, silver replicas of animals from Africa, and a silver mesh handbag from Laos are displayed beneath the beveled glass top.

The edges of this table are embellished with coins from Mexico, Peru, Argentina, Thailand, Zimbabwe, Sweden,

Germany, Austria, Latvia, the European Union, and more. The collection grew as a form of entertainment for my daughters on our trips. Later, we had belts made from some of the coins. Having lost my dad at a young age, I was always a firm believer in planting great memories. They can never be taken away from you. The coins are symbols of the adventures my children and I had together.

The move was stressful, but soon, I enjoyed sitting on my balcony, watching the runners and dog walkers below, sipping my coffee, taking great pleasure in planning the days of my new life.

In those early weeks after my return, I reveled in my newfound serenity and happiness. I had set out on my journey in search of the strong, vibrant, optimistic woman I had once been, and through spiritual and artistic growth I had found her.

Only one thing caused me a bit of concern. I tired easily, and this was new for me. Where painting once energized me, now I often felt drained. I had to rest periodically to get my strength back before I could return to my work.

I had been a healthy person all my life, favoring a nutritious diet of fresh fruits, vegetables, and seafood. I did not have a sweet tooth. When I ate a piece of chocolate or a dessert, it was always a small portion.

My healthy lifestyle extended to my choice of activities. As I child and young adult, I was a figure skater and dancer. I stopped both after my first year at Penn. Most fitness classes didn't appeal to me, but I became a yoga devotee.

My love of cooking contributed to my healthy lifestyle too. I always loved preparing interesting dinners for family and friends, trying out new recipes and replicating the dishes I loved as a child. In my travels around the world, I learned about exotic cuisines and cooking techniques that I brought home and tried out on my friends.

I had always been an active, curious, busy person. I never got bored. I never knew what being bored was, and so I attributed feeling tired and unwell to the flu or stress from the move.

For more than a year, I had traveled constantly, visiting new places and eating new foods. I had moved into and out of a large home, relocated to an apartment, and continued with my life as if I could handle it all with my usual aplomb. It had to be catching up with me, I thought.

I decided to turn to my favorite remedy for just about everything: a holiday trip. A few days free from painting and all my activities would be the best medicine for me. I felt sure that the fatigue would be gone upon my return. Traveling always invigorated me, and I refused to let a little malaise spoil my favorite holiday.

I gathered the family for Christmas in Aspen, Colorado. The picturesque setting felt like the old times, when the kids were growing up. We always decorated the house in Dallas, even though we spent the holidays in Taos, New Mexico, for many years.

Growing up with European parents in Latin America, I always had memorable holidays. I loved recreating those wonderful celebrations for my kids. When I was a child, our Christmas trees were decorated with real candles, lit every evening, creating pure magic. It is one of my fondest memories. When candles were abandoned due to safety concerns, our family did their best to replicate the little flickering flames with clear Christmas bulbs. It was never the same, but I held the memory close and continued the tradition with my own family.

When the children were little, we had two Christmas trees. One was the family tree and the other the children's tree, which they could decorate as they liked. Following the German tradition, we always made a gingerbread house decorated with candies galore.

On Christmas Eve in Taos, we watched the ski patrol descend the mountain in a lovely lantern dance before the kids went to bed to await Santa. Once the kids had fallen asleep, I set out the gifts under the tree. One year, when the twins were four and Paul was seven, I crushed up a cookie and left a trail as if Santa had done it. Andie woke her siblings up very early on Christmas morning and told them she had seen Santa and he had winked at her. Paul was skeptical until Andie showed them the cookie trail. Aina was terrified, and Paul was thrilled. Andie's story added to the electric energy of the holiday, and when the kids returned to ski school, the tale took on mythic proportions. All the kids wanted to come to our townhouse to see the cookie trail, which I was not allowed to clean up for days. Their joy delighted me. These small memories help hold us together when our hearts breaks. And all our hearts break at one time or another.

We made more memories on the ski slopes. I have skied most of my adult life, and my kids took up the sport when they were three or four years old. I love being in the mountains in the winter, when glistening snow blankets the landscape and the sky is so clear. At night, the stars you see are never ending. It is magical and majestic.

I still wasn't feeling well, but the holiday with my kids took my mind off my physical problems. I did a lot of cooking, as always. On the slopes, you get really hungry, and you imagine how wonderful the next meal will be, savoring in your mind what will be served. As I navigated moguls on my skis, in my mind I was planning the meal I would cook at the end of the day. Our dinners began late, in the Spanish tradition, and went on into the early hours. There was lots of laughter and storytelling. We were all so happy to be together again.

Aspen has many fabulous eateries, but I have always felt holidays should be celebrated at home, where the aromas of cooking fill the house. I believe in creating sense memories with food and wine. Cooking for my family and friends is one of my great passions.

I did not know how to cook when I married. Of all the many lessons my mother insisted on, cooking was not among them. Unlike my mother, I wanted to make wonderful meals for my husband and children, so I taught myself how to cook. In our many travels, I learned about the cuisines of the world, and I still incorporate foods from many cultures.

I can't imagine eating just to eat. One eats and savors what one is eating. The simplest ingredients can make a wonderful meal, especially if you add a glass of wine. I believe in using our good china and silverware every day, not just on special occasions. They help to make every meal feel special. The important thing is to pause from our busy lives and take a few moments for ourselves and those we love.

When our family gathers on Christmas, food is of paramount importance. On Christmas Eve, we eat seafood—caviar, shrimp, salmon, and cod fish cakes prepared in the Mexican-Spanish tradition. On Christmas Day we have a goose, duck, or turkey. I always reveled in the preparation and presentation of these holiday meals. All my senses came into play—taste, smell, sight, and the sounds of oohs and ahs from an appreciative audience. To lose all that never entered my mind.

S pring arrived, and with it, renewed hopes for improved health. I tried acupuncture and acupressure and got no relief. I began to take supplements, thinking my body might be lacking essential nutrients. I was losing weight even though I was eating highly nutritious meals and not cutting back on calories. I attributed my symptoms to my busy schedule. My days were packed with activities, and in the evenings, I painted. There was little time for relaxation.

I tried slowing down, but the feelings of fatigue worsened. Then it occurred to me I could be suffering from some sort of allergy. Dallas is known for its high pollen and mold counts. The city was built on prairie land, but its ecosystem has been transformed by manmade lakes and landscaping. The atmosphere has been greatly altered, too—poisoned, as a matter of fact. All of this contributes to an abnormally high incidence of allergies among Dallas residents. I felt sure this was what I was suffering from. I had experienced sinus issues thirty years earlier, when I first moved to Dallas, and I imagined the problem had recurred, especially after my long absence. Even so, I had never been so tired in my life.

I decided to see the ear, nose, and throat specialist who had done my sinus surgery two years earlier. I felt optimistic, thinking this would all be over soon, and I would get back to normal life. I expected a full allergy assessment test, but after a quick examination, my doctor suggested I do an endoscopy. I was okay with that. By then, I had a new symptom: a chronic sore throat. I was ready to do anything to get my health back.

The doctor placed a tube with a tiny camera attached to it in my mouth, which enabled him to view hidden areas all the way down my throat. After the brief procedure, he came back into the examining room with a grim look. "We need to do a biopsy," he said.

I had come for a simple allergy assessment, and now I was undergoing these other tests. What did it mean? I had no idea where this was leading. I was confused, but still fine with his suggestions. And then he said something dreadful: "I think this could be cancer. What I saw when we took the endoscopy seems like cancer."

Twice. He said the C word not once, but twice.

I looked at him, dumbfounded.

"We don't know yet, but I will be sending these biopsy results to the lab, and I will try to rush the results."

I left the office and stepped out into the bright sunshine. There wasn't a cloud in the sky. I smiled. Cancer? You have to be kidding. It struck me as funny. Obviously, my doctor didn't know that I was not the cancer type. No. Not me. I don't get cancer.

I had plans to celebrate my birthday with my girlfriends that night. The biopsy knocked me off balance, but it didn't knock me out. I love celebrations, especially birthdays, and I had no intention of missing out.

I believe every birthday is important, not just the ones everybody makes a big fuss over, like eighteen, twenty-one, thirty, fifty, and so on. Each new year of your life is a marker for how far you have come, how good you feel, and where you are headed. In my family, no matter what age you are or how rough the year has been, we celebrate. It is one of the rewards of being alive.

The girlfriends who organized my birthday dinner are the sisters I have chosen. We are very close and have been since we met in Dallas many years ago. Most of them are Mexican, and the Spanish language and the culture we all miss unites us. We have raised our children together, sharing the ups and downs of their romances, their college acceptances, their job searches, their marriages, and their divorces. We are the tías (the aunts) that solve all, and know all. Maybe we never really solve any problems. Most of them can't be avoided. They are just part of living. But we give each other full permission to vent without being judged. We love each other like family, stand by each other in our struggles, and celebrate the joys, always giving support and plenty of advice.

Our famous lunches begin around two in the afternoon and go on until ten at night or later. At big parties we have mariachis, and when the men do not want to dance, we dance with each other. And do we dance! We know how to have fun.

We are all very different, but we bring out the best in each other. For me, this is what real friendship looks like.

No matter how bad things get, these friends stay close. For instance, they had my back during one of the worst experiences of my life. Not long after my divorce, I received a call that my mother-in-law had been murdered in Mexico City. I had spoken to her the night before, just hours before the tragedy. In a haze of disbelief and shock, I handled all the details. I called my ex-husband to give him the terrible news and made travel arrangements for the whole family.

Once the adrenaline wore off, I was exhausted. Thanks to my sisters, help was on the way. News travels at lightning speed in our group. My friend Cathy heard what happened and arrived at my door unbidden, with coffee, drinks, and flowers. She helped me pack my suitcase and offered to accompany me to Mexico City for the funeral. Because of a bond created long ago, she knew exactly what I needed.

These are the friends who organized a dinner to celebrate my birthday and my new life. And these are the friends who stuck by me when my new life took a downturn.

That night, a friend hosted my birthday dinner in her home, one of the most beautiful in Dallas. She decorated her eighteen-foot-long dining table with white and brown speckled dry beans arranged in swirls and stars and hearts circling an elaborate candelabra. Candles of every shape and size lit every room and bathed the sublime art on the walls in their warm light.

Everyone contributed something to this special evening. The most beautiful thing was the love and comfort that enveloped me. The pièce de résistance brought tears to my eyes: one friend brought me a cupcake decorated with a wax bust of Frida Kahlo, whom I count as a fellow traveler in so many ways.

Frida Kahlo was a very famous Mexican painter of the mid-twentieth century. Her works were mostly intimate self-portraits inspired by fantasy, the Mexican culture, and the lifelong chronic pain she endured from injuries to her back and pelvis in a horrible accident. My friends and I all love art, especially the works of Mexican artists, so it was perfect in that way.

Hidden behind my smiles and laughter that night was the fear that Frida and I would have much more in common than our love of painting. I thought of my recent journey and how much my life had already changed. And I thought of Frida and how her entire life had been a tumultuous ride. While in San Miguel, I wrote down three quotes of hers in my journal. As I sat there among my friends, holding on to this moment of perfection in my life, Frida's words flashed across my mind: "Nothing is absolute. Everything changes, everything moves, everything flies and goes away."

I tried not to cry during this wonderful celebration, and when I did let a tear fall, I blamed it on sentimental feelings for my dear friends. I did not tell any of them about the biopsy earlier in the day. I would never have let myself turn such a happy occasion into a sad one. I had cause to celebrate, and celebrate we did. I had, after all, just returned from my fabulous trip. I had come to terms with so much and found myself again. Cancer couldn't possibly be on my horizon.

Still, Frida's words gave me pause. They seemed somehow prophetic, as if all the change I had experienced on my journey marked the beginning, not the end, of my transformation. I looked at my Frida cupcake and thought of her valiant battles with pain and her tumultuous life with her husband, Diego Rivera. I am by no means as talented as Frida, nor have I faced the severe pain she lived with for decades. But I am inspired by her ability to express her emotions in her work. I feared I would soon walk in her shoes, and hoped I, too, would rise to the occasion and make art out of my troubles.

I ate the cupcake and took home the wax bust of Frida. Late that night, I wept from fear as I put her on my desk. Titan, alarmed at my emotional state, consoled me with kisses. Unable to sleep, I rose early the next morning and took a long walk with him. I savored the smell of spring in the air. Afterward, I meditated and prayed that I would understand what was happening to me and make peace with it.

I spent the rest of the morning packing for a flight to Charleston, South Carolina. Andie and Aina planned to meet me there for a special birthday weekend. Then the phone rang.

The doctor's nurse told me the results were back and the doctor wanted to see me as soon as possible. I knew I couldn't go on the trip with my kids with such a huge cloud hanging over me. I needed answers. I needed to know what the future held.

Racing over to the doctor's office, I combed over the possibilities. Wouldn't he have told me I was fine over the phone? Why tell me to come over if it wasn't serious? I felt scared but hopeful that he had been mistaken in his suspicions.

Time slowed down to a tortuous crawl as I waited for the doctor and his verdict. The room seemed overly stuffy and hot. My stomach quaked. I imagined I could see my heart pounding beneath my crisp white shirt.

"As I suspected, you have tongue cancer squamous cell carcinoma."

His voice echoed through a thick fog. My mind went blank for a second before I could get a grasp on my senses. I saw the doctor's face across the desk, and then I didn't. I heard his words, and then I questioned whether I had.

Denial swept in to rescue me. He had to be joking. The results had to be wrong.

He talked to me about my condition, but all I heard was one word. Cancer. Cancer. Cancer.

The slayer had come knocking on my door, and I had let the monster in.

I felt I could disintegrate right there in his mahogany and leather chair. I wanted to cry, to scream out, to unleash my fury against whomever or whatever had allowed this to happen to me.

But no. I was brought up to tough out the worst. I didn't do any of that. Not then. I kept my composure and listened to every impossible word the doctor uttered.

"I have set you up for a CT scan. You have to do it quickly so we can assess the stage of the cancer. We have to act fast. You have an appointment next week with Dr. Lance Oxford, the best head and neck surgeon in the country. I would choose him if I were in your shoes."

I needed an ally, someone who would keep all this information straight. Who knew? I could be hallucinating. This could be a very bad dream. Nevertheless, I went through the motions. I did as I was told, as if this was real. I had the CT scan done immediately. And then I drove myself home.

I navigated downtown Dallas in shock. I had cancer! Not just any cancer. Tongue cancer. Men get tongue cancer. Not women. Why me? I never even heard of it. Cancer of the oral cavity?

At a stoplight, I touched my finger to the soft pink cushion that licked ice cream cones when I was little and turned dark from sipping red wine. My tongue, friend to the sensual delights I cherished, transformed with the doctor's words into an enemy poised to kill me.

I tried to talk myself out of what I had just been told. I cannot have cancer, I muttered out loud. I live a healthy life. Even as a child, I strived for balance and watched my choices. I reminded myself that I haven't eaten processed food in years. I've never smoked, and I'm not a heavy drinker. I've never had a major illness. I rarely even catch cold.

It definitely has to be a wrong diagnosis, I said to myself. I know something is wrong with me, but it's not cancer.

I thought about my spiritual seeking and the energetic work I had done with Lupita. Surely, this rendered me immune to this, the worst diagnosis I could imagine. I lived life to the fullest. I didn't sit around and worry about tomorrow. I did yoga and meditated. I had devoted myself to my idea of physical and spiritual perfection with the determination my mother had applied to perfecting me in her image. Surely this bought me a pass.

I was not the typical cancer person, I told myself. How then could this happen to me? There had been no history of cancer in my family, so why now? Between bouts of crying, I looked at myself in the mirror. I looked remarkably fit for my age. Inside and out, I presented the picture of health. My body was not an open invitation to cancer!

The truth is, there's no such thing as a typical cancer patient. Cancer is an equal-opportunity giver. It can attack anyone. But I wasn't ready to entertain that notion. My first and natural reaction was denial.

Anger followed close on on the heels of denial. It rose in me, bitter as bile. Life is unfair, I said to my reflection in the glass. You give so much to life and you end up with this. I clung to denial and gave in to rage, but the pain continued to pound me with the truth: I had cancer.

S unglasses disguised the shock and grief in my puffy red eyes as I drove to the airport. I had called my children with the news, and I had insisted we would go ahead with our plans for a fun-filled weekend in Charleston.

Someone else might have canceled this trip, but that wasn't me. Even in my shock, fear, and anger at the injustice of the diagnosis, I had my boxing gloves on. I had no intention of letting cancer take me down.

We all needed the weekend together. More than anything, I wanted to be surrounded by my children and to enjoy a brief reprieve from what I knew would be a long and difficult ordeal. Travels and celebrations have always made me smile. Whenever I am down, they uplift me. I needed that at that moment in my life. Besides, who knew when I would have the opportunity to travel again?

My children met me at the airport in Charleston. We all got teary as we held each other in a group hug. I didn't want to talk about it, but they are my family, and we needed to get it all out on the table. Cancer was an interloper, an uninvited guest on our holiday, and there was no getting around the elephant in the room. It had to be accommodated.

I am very lucky to have three loving children who are always willing to drop anything when one of us is in need of family. Aina and Andie, who were twenty-five when I was diagnosed, had lived in New York since graduating from college, where Andie studied marketing and Aina international relations. Though they are identical twins, they are very different. Nevertheless, they have a bond that is greater than a sisterly bond and deep affection for one another. Their relationship has roller coaster moments, but they are fiercely protective of each other, and God help anyone who interferes or judges either one.

Their brother, Paul, who is four years older, has always been very independent. True to his nature, he lives in Mexico. He tried to work with his dad, and so did Andie and Aina, but none of them appreciated the amount of control their dad exercised over their lives. Before long, Paul established his own business, and the girls began new careers in New York. Their dad lost three very capable employees who would have had his back.

Wisdom does not necessarily come with age. I am reminded of a favorite quote from Hermann Hesse's *Siddhartha*: "Wisdom is not communicable. The wisdom which a wise man tries to communicate sounds foolish. … Knowledge can be communicated not wisdom. One can find it, live it, but one cannot communicate and teach it."

Yes, indeed.

In different ways, at different times, each of my children has fought against being controlled, just as I refused to allow my parents to control me. After the struggles with their dad, they went off to live their lives on their own terms.

I am immensely proud of each one. They chose their own paths, taking time to concentrate on themselves and figure out what they wanted. I cannot say I was as advanced in those skills at their age. It took me a lot longer to find my own way. Like me, they love life, travel, and languages. Most importantly, they love themselves, and they love others in a healthy way.

That night over dinner, I told them everything the doctor had told me, which wasn't much. At the time, I didn't know the procedures I would undergo or my chances of getting rid of it. All I really knew was that I had cancer of the tongue.

The kids wanted reassurance. "It has to be a relatively early stage, right?" I didn't have the answer to that, but I agreed. I mean, how could it be advanced?

The conversation put us all in a downcast mood, and I didn't like it. "Let's stop it, now," I said. "We will be hopeful. It's cancer. Many people have had it and lived. I will survive too. We didn't come all this way to be weepy and moody. I insist that we have a good time!"

I have always been a firm believer in living fully in the moment. My motto is, "No regrets." And so, I enjoyed our weekend immensely even though I was not my normal energetic self.

My loving children didn't fail me. Together we put the cloud behind us and made it a memorable weekend. We laughed and had a wonderful time exploring Charleston and Savannah. We stayed at a small boutique hotel overlooking a park and ate wonderful meals, visited galleries, and enjoyed the lovely weather.

By the end of the weekend, we had buoyed each other's spirits. We decided it couldn't be that bad and talked each other into being hopeful. I didn't want to leave them, and that last night with them, lying awake as they slept, I thought of my dad and how much I missed him.

I was twenty-one years old when he died, and he was fifty. I had three younger siblings. The baby was ten at the time. His death taught me that life is fragile, but I also learned to live every moment to the fullest. That was the final gift my dad gave to me.

From the day he died onward, I lived with no regrets and no unfinished business. I always told those dearest to me how much I loved them. And yet, on the day I was told I had cancer, all that wisdom went out the window. I needed more time. Even with my full life, I wanted more from this earthly existence. I wasn't nearly ready to let go.

My symptoms had worsened over the weekend. No matter how I tried to push this out of my mind, every time I swallowed, it hurt, and eating had become more uncomfortable. I knew I had to be hopeful, but the realist in me intruded. I could not run away even if I wanted to. I intended to land in Dallas and face whatever might come.

L ong before I met Lupita, I embraced meditation as central to my sense of well-being and ability to cope with whatever the universe placed in my path. I started practicing meditation years before, in Thailand, and continued my studies of this ancient practice on our trips to Laos, Cambodia, and Myanmar—places where meditation is embedded in the culture.

In those cultures, the sight of Buddhist monks dressed in their beautiful saffron robes and nuns in pink and orange is taken for granted. As they sit in deep meditation in the temples, nothing can disturb them from their inner focus. How fascinating that they can be at such peace when their countries are riddled with strife. If only I could achieve this state, I thought at the time. I am not there yet, but I have made a lot of progress in that direction, and this has served me well during my illness and recovery.

All forms of meditation guide the practitioner to presence in the moment. Transcendental meditation, which I also studied, teaches one to transcend thought and enter into pure awareness. As you repeat a mantra, you concentrate on the breath and quiet the mind. With practice, all forms of meditation offer tremendous relief from stress and anxiety.

Although I had a practiced meditation for many years, I did not achieve true peace with myself until I worked with Lupita. From her I learned how one thinks determines how one lives. Meditation trains the mind to focus on the positive. In Western cultures, we are not taught this method of dealing with suffering. Instead, our minds attach to the problems in front of us. We choose negativity when we could be choosing positivity and gratitude.

Working with Lupita, I finally got it. I had the "Aha!" moment when I understood and embraced what I had been told over and over: let go of past hurts, past conflicts, past people. You cannot feed your history and your destiny at the same time. It is natural to remember a painful, negative event, but it is in our power to decide to dwell on it or switch the channel and focus on the positive. Many say that "our thoughts become our reality."

The morning of my appointment with the specialist, I meditated. I invited only positive thoughts through gratitude for my blessings, and I let negativity flow away from me. In my meditation, I created a space for peace. By the time I left the house, the fear had subsided. Using all the tools I had learned, I prepared for the next chapter of my life.

D r. Lance Oxford, a head and neck cancer specialist, sat across from me. I trembled and tightened my grip on a thin thread of hope.

Then the doctor lowered the boom.

With a sad smile, he said, "I am really sorry about the state you're in. From going through your records, you seem quite healthy, but cancer has a way of creeping into people's lives."

His mouth kept moving, but my mind could only process the big question hanging between us like the blade of a guillotine: what stage?

"…stage four cancer."

What? Did he say stage four cancer? "Did you say stage four?"

"I'm afraid so," he said. "We don't know yet how far it has spread. That's why we have to do the procedures as soon as possible."

His words roared like a freight train bearing down on me. I froze in its blinding lights. Shaken and shivering, I struggled to regain control of myself.

He prattled on as if I could hear him, as if any words beyond "stage four" had any meaning. I do recall that he closed our meeting with a ray of hope.

"The peculiar thing about tongue cancer is that it varies in each case," he said. "There is a good success rate for being cancer-free."

I had already done the research. I knew. Stage four is the final stage. There is no stage five. It means the cancer has spread to other organs. It means you could die.

The knowledge shattered my inner calm. But meditation has turned my mind into a positivity-seeking missile. My thoughts latched on to the doctor's last words: I am sure we can work together in making you well again. What that work might entail, I had yet to learn.

E ven with the die cast, I asked for a rescan, holding on to hope that there had been a mistake. A part of me still didn't believe I had cancer. I mean, life was going so well. I was just beginning to discover myself. I nurtured my positive attitude and practiced daily gratitude. How, then, could something this bad happen to me?

And yet, the rescans confirmed that, indeed, stage four tongue cancer was happening to me.

I trusted Dr. Oxford, but after talking it over with my kids, we decided we must get a second opinion before submitting to such drastic procedures. We sent my test results to other doctors. However, all our inquiries led to one conclusion. Dr. Oxford's colleagues in the field considered him the best for my type of cancer. They reassured us I was in good hands.

Dr. Oxford's team approach is integral to his high success rate. He assembles a team of rock stars that encompasses the treatments from surgery to the final stages of recovery. From the time I signed on with him, I never had to make another decision about my care. He hand-picked the oncologist, the radiologist, the plastic surgeon, all the therapists, including the lymphedema and speech therapists, and even a dentist who specializes in post-radiation dentistry. All of my appointments were scheduled for me for the entire treatment program. I never had to think about anything but staying positive and getting well.

My children remained staunchly supportive during this critical time. Together, we educated and prepared for what I was going to undergo. I am a firm believer in a holistic approach, but in this case, being holistic was not an option by itself. It could only complement the procedures recommended by my doctors. I already had a Fentanyl patch for the pain. Soon, the suffering would border on the unendurable. We had to act fast.

Dr. Oxford and Dr. Jason Potter, the plastic surgeon responsible for the reconstruction of my tongue, laid out the treatment plan. I would undergo a partial glossectomy. Then my tongue would be rebuilt with tissue from my forearm, and tissue from my upper leg would replace what was taken from my arm. Some of my lymph nodes would also be removed. These are small bean-shaped glands that produce and house lymphocytes and filter microorganisms and other particles, thus reducing the risk of infection. They are critical to the functioning of the immune system, and a tracheotomy was the only way to get at the ones that needed to go. Radiation and chemotherapy would follow the surgery as soon as I regained some of my strength.

For an unspecified period, all my nutrients would come from a feeding tube inserted directly into my stomach. It would take months of healing and intensive muscle training for my new tongue before I would swallow normally or speak again.

The timetable left no opportunity to ponder. In my view, I had only two choices. Each one demanded a gambler's nerve. I could do nothing, live in pain, and die a painful death within the next several months, or I could give Dr. Oxford's proposed treatment plan a try. It would be extremely invasive, and I would face a long recovery. I would lose my ability to speak, my sense of taste, my swallow reflex, and consequently, my ability to eat. I would be bedridden for weeks, maybe months, and long after, I would experience muscle weakness and fatigue. With all that, I stood a chance of surviving, of living pain-free, of going on to experience more adventures and, God willing, staying alive for my children. The choice appeared frightening and obvious.

I told the doctor I would go ahead with the treatment he recommended. He nodded and told me I had little time to act. From diagnosis to surgery, I had less than a month.

The decision to go ahead with Dr. Oxford's treatment plan took all the strength and courage I had in me. I thought about the fire in Barcelona. For the second time in a year, I was being called upon to take a leap of faith. I remembered looking down on the firefighters below. The mattress they held looked like a tiny target against a background of sure death. And yet, I had dropped Titan to save him, and I had jumped to save myself.

Alone at home, I broke down and cried like never before. None of the painful events in my life prepared me for this coming showdown with cancer.

I cried all that day, grieving for the carefree life I might never regain. I wanted everything to go back to how it was. I wanted to be whole again and free from the cancer. Over and over, I asked God what I had done to make this happen to me.

The procedures scared me almost as much as the disease that, left untreated, would surely kill me. I knew many people had gone through these treatments and had not survived. Some survived only to have the cancer return. I knew I could be facing the same fate.

I missed my children and longed for someone to talk to, someone to assure me that I was going to be all right, that I would pull through. And yet, I didn't reach out. I sensed the importance of sitting alone with my fears in order to purge them. I was letting go of the heartache and preparing emotionally for the challenges ahead of me. All the pain I had stored deep inside poured out. By day's end, I had passed through that wall of anger, denial, and grief. Cleansed of these negative energies, I was, ready to face whatever the future might hold with a positive attitude.

I called my friends to break the sad news to them. Of course, they offered every form of support I could possibly need. But I knew I needed more than even they could provide. I needed Lupita.

She had already done hypnosis sessions with me over the past year. When we weren't communicating by phone, I listened to the recordings she made for me. Working with her, I always felt calm and grounded. I knew she would help me find the needed strength and belief in a good outcome.

As soon as I heard Lupita's voice, I broke down. "I have cancer," I said. "Of the tongue."

"What stage?" she asked.

"Stage four." Once again it sounded unbelievable in my ears, but it was what it was.

I told her about the procedures that would likely save me and admitted how much they scared me.

She told me to calm down. "Everything will be all right," she said. "There is no need to cry or fret. You have cancer. It drains the body of life force. We just have to focus on how to get rid of it and move on."

Lupita then explained something that became very evident to me as the months wore on. "Cancer drains not only physically, but spiritually and emotionally," she said. "In many cases, it isn't the cancer that kills it is the loss of will. People lose strength and hope. Often the body is treated, and the soul is ignored. You could be getting cured of the cancer, but if your soul is weak, you could still die."

I knew she was right, but I was not at all sure my soul was up to the challenge.

"Here is what we're going to do," she said. "While the doctors take care of your body, you will train your soul and make it stronger. That's how you will conquer this cancer."

That very day, we began the sessions that saw me through the cancer treatment and recovery. Lupita wasted no time in getting to the crux of the matter.

"I know you know why you got cancer of the oral cavity."

In those first days after the diagnosis, denial, anger, and resentment at the injustice of it consumed me. But even then, I heard the whisper of the truth. Behind "why me" was an answer I did not want to hear.

"You have to face the truth before surgery," she said. "If you don't, you won't make it."

In the long silence that followed, I quieted my mind, stilled the inner chatter, and focused on my breath. Before long, the truth made itself known to me. "I did not communicate my real feelings," I said. "I did not speak my truth."

"And what is that truth?" she asked.

"For nearly thirty years, I held on to the façade that kept my marriage going. I refused to express my real self."

Most of us are good at hiding layers of self. We're afraid to take the risk of presenting our authentic selves to the world. We develop coping mechanisms to deal with the crazies in our lives, the traumas, and the losses. In the process, we shut up bits and pieces of our real selves, those parts that rock the boat. My mother did it. Her mother probably did it. And much as I didn't want to repeat my mother's mistakes, I did it too.

I feel sure that I did not pass this family karma on to my daughters. We always had honest relationships with each

Photo Album

Mom and Me in New York City in 1958.

Dinner with my parents at Las Brisas Acapulco in 1964 . My love of Mexico had already begun.

Hostal de la Gavina S'Agaro in Spain, 1970.

At the end of my freshman year at the University of Pennsylvania in 1974.

My Ketty, Madrid, Spain, in 1964.

The beautiful home I built post divorce in 2010 (and sold in 2014).

The pool, 2010.

The kitchen, 2010.

The family room, 2010.

"Frida Kahlo Cupcake." My birthday
Celebration with my girlfriends, 2015.

The living room, 2010.

Paul and me in Munich, Germany, in 1989.

Spring Break with my children in Osaka, Nara, and Kyoto, Japan in 1997.

Lugano, Switzerland, where Paul, Aina, and Andie attended school from 2003–2004.

Galapagos, Ecuador, with my children in 1999.

Angkor Wat, Cambodia, in 2000.   Klosters, Switzerland, in 2004.

Summer in Thailand with Paul, Aina, and Andie in 2000.

Visit to Latvia and to my mother's country home. "Udensdzirnavas," 2008.

Paul and me on a stop in Santa Fe on our way to Taos in 2000.

"Eat, Paint, Love" journey continues   Aspen, Colorado, in 2014.
in Santa Fe, New Mexico, 2013.

Gordes Castle, Luberon, France,   Safari, Kruger National Park in
in 1998.   1997.

Christmas with Aina, Andie, and Titan, San Miguel Allende, Mexico, 2015.

Skiing with my children at Christmastime in 1994.

White Rock Lake after a walk with Titan in Dallas, Texas, in 2012.

Me during my chemo and radiation treatments with Paul, Dallas, Texas, 2015.

Starting my "birthday" celebrations with Titan, who will have some cake! 2012.

Santa Fe, New Mexico, "Eat, Paint, Love" journey, 2013.

Jardin de Luxembourg , Paris, France, "Eat, Paint, Love" journey, 2013.

Paris, France, with Titan during my "Eat, Paint, Love" journey, 2013.

Paul and Titan as my "Eat, Paint, Love" journey is about to start, Dallas, Texas, in 2012.

"Eat, Paint, Love" journey,
Barcelona, Spain, 2013.

Ready for my birthday celebrations
during my "Eat, Paint, Love"
journey in Barcelona, Spain, 2013.

"Eat, Paint, Love" journey go-karts Barcelona, Spain, 2013.

Santa Fe, New Mexico, "Eat,
Paint, Love" journey, 2012.

Return to Dallas following my "Eat,
Paint, Love" journey, 2014.

Santa Fe, New Mexico, with Aina, 2013.

New York, New York, Happy Birthday Twinkie, "Eat, Paint, Love," 2013.

Visit by Aina and Andie in San Miguel Allende, Mexico, in 2013 during my "Eat, Paint, Love" journey.

Paris, France, with Titan Trocadéro during my "Eat, Paint, Love" journey, 2013.

Tablescapes of Las Frutas, painted in Barcelona, Spain, 2013.

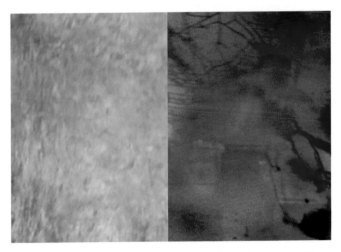

Inner Emotions of the Mind, *The Fire of Barcelona*, painted in
painted in Barcelona, Spain, 2013. San Miguel Allende, Mexico, 2013.

other. I taught them to do what I did not do for myself: "You must know yourself to find the right partner in life."

When I set out on my journey the year before, I thought reclaiming my independent, creative self would bring me the freedom and happiness I sought. But the universe said no, not so fast. It brought me cancer. My trial by fire. To survive it meant resurrecting my deepest, truest self.

The news of my cancer diagnosis spread like wildfire. My phone rang continuously with people calling to check up on me. The love and support of my friends overwhelmed me. I heard from people I had not talked to in ages. Even though my body grew weaker daily, each call made me feel a little bit stronger and more determined to beat this thing. Their love made me hold on to hope.

Even so, I was having doubts at this stage. In my darkest moments, I feared I would not survive. People told me this, too, would pass, but with the amount of pain I was experiencing, I sometimes believed otherwise. I still had so much I wanted to do, but cancer had stopped me in my tracks. Would I ever get up again?

Preparing for the worst, I tied up loose ends. I counted myself lucky to have an opportunity to settle my affairs. Some never get the chance and leave much undone. I met with my attorney to set my will in order. I wrote copious instructions regarding my finances and other details of my life. I wanted everything to be clear. My children didn't deserve to inherit a mess.

As I prepared for what was to come, it all began to sink in, and the fear became nearly unmanageable. With the increasing pain, I thought I didn't stand a chance. At times, I counted every breath as if it might be my last. Negative thoughts cluttered my mind. It was not like me to let them take over. But I think the negativity hastened the weakening of my system. Lupita and I had work to do and a very short time to do it. June 22 was less than two weeks away.

5

*At the end of the day, we can endure much
more than we think we can.*

—Frida Kahlo

My children arrived in Dallas on June 20. I told myself
I would not cry, but having them by my side as I
prepared for the Monday-morning surgery touched me
deeply. Their presence comforted me. We parents naturally
want to comfort our children. Circumstances don't usually
call for the other way around. Thank God I raised them to
be compassionate, loving people. Our united front against
the cancer buoyed my spirits. My confidence in a future
returned, though what that future might look like still
frightened me.

Lupita and I had worked on lessening my fears through
hypnosis, and those sessions had helped a lot. I was in a
miserable state at that point. Every day the pain in my

mouth grew worse, and my body weakened. In a matter of weeks, I had dropped fourteen pounds, from 123 to 109.

My children and I tried to cheer ourselves up, but we were all gloomy. They tried to hide it, but I could see the worry in their eyes. They were scared of losing me, and I worried about what would happen to them if I died. I looked at the three of them and hid my tears. I knew I had done well in bringing them up, but I wondered how they would survive without me and how my death would affect them. When I lost my father, I felt alone and angry at the world, and I wanted to spare them from such suffering.

Before going to bed, I spoke with each of them separately, knowing that for many months, I would be unable to speak at all. That I might die remained unsaid but lurked in the background. We hugged and headed for restless sleep with heavy hearts.

June 22, 2015, arrived just like any other summer day in Texas. The air had not cooled much below eighty degrees. I awoke before dawn to the sound of birds chirping in the trees outside my window. Brushing my teeth, I stuck out my tongue and looked at my reflection. I shivered. Goodbye, tongue.

The rest of Dallas still slept as Paul drove us down to Baylor on the empty streets. The surgery had been scheduled for early in the morning to make time for the long procedure.

Looking at their forced smiles and teary eyes, it occurred to me I might never see them again. Then I shook that negative thinking off and held, instead, onto hope. As Lupita taught me, I made my affirmations: I will live. I will not die. Everything will go according to plan. Soon I will start doing what I love and be with those I love.

"I love you all," I told my children. "Be strong and hopeful. I will see you in a bit."

The surgery began at 10:00 a.m. and lasted for more than ten hours. At some point that night, I awoke in the ICU. I lingered in consciousness for only a few moments, long enough to see my children's frightened faces. I held their gaze, willing them to see my abiding love for them.

The next day, the drugs wore off enough for me to remain conscious for more than a few moments. I was completely immobilized. My body felt alien from my self, as if a heavy and immovable steel object had replaced it. All I could do was stare out from inside this shell that imprisoned me. I formed the word hello in my mind, but my mouth did not open. My breath did not tickle my throat with the aitch sound. The tip of my tongue did not touch the roof of my mouth for the l's. Words failed me.

Yes, I had been prepared for this, and yet, like the death of a loved one, I was not ready for it. Being rendered mute sent me into a tailspin. My brain worked perfectly. I formed the words in my mind. But my body did not obey the impulse. I thought I might have squeezed the pump too often and fallen into a morphine-induced dream. Encased in my utter silence, I felt frightened and alone.

My daughter Andie had foreseen this problem. She bought a dry erase board and set it up near my bed. The following day, when I could move my arms, I started using it to communicate with the nurses. In the ensuing months, I wielded my pen like a pro, dashing down words quickly, and engaging in full conversations. But in those first days, when I could barely move, my only tool for communication felt clumsy and slow.

My left arm and leg were bandaged where the tissue was grafted. My neck hurt. My mouth hurt. Everything hurt.

Morphine provided relief, but sometimes, no amount of the drug could kill the pain. The only comfort I felt was the presence of my children, who stayed with me around the clock.

In those first days, I incessantly questioned my decision to have the surgery. I feared the pain would never leave me, and my quality of life would never improve. I hated the ICU and the total confinement to bed. I had spent my life traveling the world. I spoke four languages—more if you count the ones I know well enough to get by. And here I lay 24/7, unable to move or speak.

My daughters, who were always with me, intuited my every need. They covered me with a blanket when I felt cold and raised my bed up and down when I wanted to change position. My daily activity was limited to watching movies. The rest of the time, I slept. Aina and Andie chose comedies to lighten the mood. I'm sure it helped, but I do not remember any of them. Sleep became my refuge. Only then could I get a break from thinking about my condition and my future.

I transferred to a regular room after a week in the ICU. Just when I thought things were looking up, they connected a feeding tube to my stomach. The tube carried specially formulated liquid nutrients that replaced all the wonderful foods I once enjoyed.

There is nothing quite like watching every meal travel the length of a tube that empties directly into your stomach. No savory or sweet washing over taste buds, activating salivary glands. No crunch. No creamy. No chewy. Nothing passing over the newly constructed tongue laying on the bed of my mouth like sleeping beauty. Our bodies aren't designed for this mechanical bypass of the digestive system, so my stomach often rejected the shakes.

I could not even drink water. It might seem like the easiest thing to swallow, but in fact, it is easy to aspirate, making it one of the most difficult liquids to drink. Until my mouth, my tongue, and my throat healed considerably, I had to be hydrated through an IV.

When I felt brave enough to look at myself in the mirror, I saw someone stripped of many human qualities, an object with a tube protruding from its stomach. This was not the body I knew, the one I had cared for and kept strong and limber. A thin stranger with heavy eyes and cheeks drained of color replaced the outer self I had come to like.

Yet, I knew this was me. My soul resided in this new shell. I would learn to nurture it, work with it, retrain it to become, once again, the strong, proud body that carried my children, explored the world, sat in silent meditation. I vowed I would regain what I had lost. But I knew this would take time. I had to learn to be patient and endure.

Determined to begin my recovery immediately, I started taking a few steps before the doctors and nurses approved.

With my monitors hooked to me, I walked the long, wide hallways of the hospital. I knew movement was important to hasten my healing and avoid atrophy. The last thing I wanted was to use a walker or a wheelchair. I wanted to stand on my own.

The feeding tube made walking quite painful, but I had taken aim at a goal. Although I was often overwhelmed with frustration, I kept moving and walking despite the pain. One day a very kind and perceptive nurse gave me a small stone inscribed with the words "one step at a time". I cherished this gift. Whenever I got frustrated, I held it and remembered to take it easy.

M oving one step at a time, I hastened my transfer to the rehabilitation unit after less than a month in the hospital. There, in addition to physical therapy, I began therapy for lymphedema, which is edemic swelling caused when the flow of lymphatic fluid is interrupted by the removal of the lymph nodes. All that fluid retention in my neck made me look like a creature in a scary movie. The therapist told me this condition has no cure. My mind refused to process that information. Sometimes, we simply can't allow the word *no* to enter our consciousness.

My spirits got an extra boost on the day Titan came to stay with me in the rehab hospital. Andie and Aina had seen how lonesome he was for me. In my absence, he had become depressed and stopped eating. When they snuck Titan into my room, he leaped for me as soon as he saw me. His sad moans told me he hated the state I was in. I hated it more. We had traveled almost everywhere together, and I had missed him terribly. As soon as we were reunited, he cheered up, and so did I. All was right with the world again.

Titan stayed in the room with me for the duration of my stay. The nursing staff never realized he was a real dog. He lay very still by my side, and they thought he was a stuffed animal until the day I was discharged, when he trotted past the nurse's station by my side.

My children continued to stay with me during the entire course of my hospitalization. They were the only ones who were allowed to see me. My depleted immune system required a sort of quarantine that limited visitation even during rehabilitation, which lasted more than three weeks.

Though they couldn't see me, my many dear friends called and emailed with prayers and messages of love and support. I received gifts and flowers every day, enough to fill the room many times over. One day Aina counted seventy arrangements. By evening I had eighty. The flower deliveries continued during my entire stay. It was the closest I came to nature for all those weeks, and it made me smile.

My friends ensured that my children could concentrate on my care, sending meals and groceries to the apartment. They coddled and loved Aina, Andie, and Paul, for whom it was a difficult time. I often heard from friends that my children handled my illness incredibly well, especially considering they had never experienced this type of challenge. One rarely has experience to prepare for these tragedies, but I like to think that my children imitated what they witnessed growing up. They were nurtured and cared for throughout their childhoods, and they learned how to give that kind of care in return.

Having my children with me made all the difference in my recovery. I never felt abandoned or alone. Loneliness is something to avoid as a cancer patient. It makes you feel down and hopeless. Surrounded by love, you realize life is worth fighting for.

Andie quit her job to come take care of me. Aina flew to Dallas every weekend to give her sister a rest. No matter how kind and caring the hospital staff is, patients need advocates, and they were mine. Paul flew in often and took care of me in ways that I would not have expected him to ever do. This attentive care from my children continued when I went home. I am very lucky to have this consistent support. I would not have recovered as quickly without them.

During this time I practiced daily meditation and continued the work I had begun with Lupita in the area of energy and positivity. Our recorded telephone sessions healed my spirit even as my body struggled. Her soothing voice prompted me to close my eyes and focus on a particular aspect of my pain or healing. Sometimes I listened to the tapes subliminally as I slept.

Some of my friends were skeptical about my work with Lupita, while others believed. I only cared that it worked for me. I was healing, and though the slowness and difficulty of the process frustrated me at times, I never fell into the black hole of depression. I have witnessed that descent in others, and I am hypervigilant about avoiding it.

Unable to swallow, speak, and move—and disfigured as I was—the monster, depression, lurked in the shadows. I had to mount a strong defense. Lupita's recordings helped immensely. They set my mind at peace and gave me hope. Every session ended with positivity. Her subliminal messages encouraged me to trust myself and believe in a good outcome. I learned to act "as if." For instance, I would act as if my mouth was healing even if it didn't feel like it was, and I would act as if I felt better when in truth, I felt perfectly awful.

Many might smirk at this esoteric practice, but I have found that subliminal messages work. We are made up of energy, and energy profoundly affects us. I feel very strongly that I was able to control my fear because of Lupita's tapes. The energy work with her was a key component of my accelerated recovery.

One day, working with Lupita on the phone, I visualized myself completely healed. I came out of that session very upbeat and ready to take a walk down the hallway. My body still ached, and I was still plugged into all sorts of IVs and other contraptions. I ignored my present reality and pushed on, tubes and wires dangling by my side.

That evening the nurse took my vitals. I was fine. After saying good night to Aina, who slept on the other bed, I closed my eyes and started meditating. Soon I entered into a tranquil state. I felt amazingly light and then experienced a sense of floating. My focus shifted, and I observed myself and my daughter from a distance above us. I tried to scream but, as in a nightmare, nothing came out.

I remained calm for the first moments, but as I continued to observe from outside myself, I began to fear I would not get back to my body. I tried to scream again, and again nothing came out. Though I remained calm, I desperately wanted Aina to wake up. In my altered state, I forgot I could not speak, and I wanted to talk to her. Helpless to alter anything from this different plane of reality, I could only watch her sleeping peacefully, unaware of my predicament.

Suddenly, I heard the crash of the TV remote control. I do not know how it fell to the floor, but the clatter awakened Aina.

"Mumsie, are you okay?" she said.

Simultaneously, the alarm on one of my monitors, and then another, went off. How I observed all of this I do not know. What I do remember is seeing everything clearly and feeling calm. The alarm broke the spell. I returned to my body and awoke.

The nurses came running. My blood pressure had risen and my temperature had spiked. I explained to Aina on the white board what had occurred. She informed Lupita, who believed I had had an out-of-body experience. I had never heard of such a thing, much less experienced it myself, and it has never happened again.

In rehab, I learned to take care of my feeding tube and feed myself with it. I hated the thing protruding from my stomach, making me look and feel like some kind of Frankenstein. The tube had to be kept clean to prevent infections. At the time I thought this would be a temporary inconvenience. Little did I know I would be attached to this contraption for over seven months.

Despite the feeding tube, I was determined to get up and move. I took it one step at a time as the nurse had suggested. Soon I progressed to a walk down a few feet of hallway, and then a complete circuit around the floor of the rehab unit. Every day I added another step. I walked the halls several times a day, wheeling the pole that carried my monitors and IVs. I practiced my speech constantly, exercising my tongue to form consonants and vowels. Being an extremely active participant in my rehabilitation definitely contributed to my successful recovery.

Near the end of my hospital stay, I realized I had lost track of the weeks. My room and the hallways contained my entire reality. I lived outside of time, keenly focused on my visualizations of a pain-free, healed body. I noticed I no longer harbored any fears or anger. I no longer tortured myself by asking, why did this happen to me? Yes it was painful, but I chose to muster my inner strength and react from a positive stance. You cannot control adversity, only how you react to it. Wasting time and energy on being angry struck me as irrelevant. Cancer had happened, and there was no going back. I concentrated on getting well and being fully alive again.

M y stay in the hospital and rehabilitation lasted over six weeks. Sometime around August 11, I finally returned home. My weight had dropped even further, to 105 pounds. Although my nurses and doctors had been wonderful, I was thrilled to be out of there. I just wanted to be back in familiar surroundings and the comfort of my own bed.

In my rush to escape my claustrophobic room, the institutional hallways, and those machines attached to me, I left with an IV still in my arm. We all laughed as I sheepishly walked down that hall one more time for the final, official disconnect.

6

Mirror mirror on the wall, I'll always get up after I fall. And whether I run, walk, or have to crawl, I'll set my goals and achieve them all.

—Chris Butler

The surgery and rehab left me weakened but unbowed. With my return home, I had reached a major milestone. I welcomed this next phase, which I saw as a move toward normalcy. Although I was pretty much confined to my bedroom, I had Titan with me, and I was surrounded by my art and mementos and all the things I cherished. Reminders of my travels brought me great pleasure and hope for future trips. I thought of San Miguel when I looked at the antique carved Mexican doors hung on each side of my bed. Centered above the headboard, a painting depicting the Lake District in Italy took me back to one of my favorite destinations.

I had to continue my quarantine at home. Any exposure to viruses or germs would have caused serious damage to my health. As much as I wanted to see everyone, I couldn't risk that, so I limited my visitors to two of my "sisters." This helped to protect my immune system, and I also felt reluctant to show my disfigured face. Going through that over and over, as each new friend came by, would have been very difficult for me.

I had full-time help, as I was too weak to do much of anything. Twice a week, a nurse came to change the bandages on my graft wounds to ensure they healed properly. My kids continued to take turns staying with me, and though I loved having them, as I began to regain some strength, I became more frustrated at my lack of independence. I had done things by myself all my life, and now I couldn't. I could not turn my head, so driving was not possible. I thought often about the quality of life I could expect, and I wondered if I would ever recover fully and be able to do the things I liked.

When I looked in the mirror, I saw a skeleton, not the toned and fit athletic body I always had. With only two weeks before chemotherapy and radiation, I wanted to retain my weight and, hopefully, to gain some. The treatments would drain me, and I needed every pound I could get to build my strength and boost my immune system. I was still trying to get a hang of my feeding tube, learning how to feed myself those shakes, which were my only nourishment. I don't know how I was supposed to gain weight on this liquid diet, but there was no alternative. I slowed down to a crawl to avoid expending calories and spent my days at rest, watching television, meditating, and sleeping as much as possible.

The tracheotomy tube was removed when I left the hospital, which meant I could start speech therapy. My therapist was a chipper young woman who looked to me like she had never had a care in the world. By the third session, I took my frustration and self-pity out on her when she asked me once again to do the impossible with my new tongue.

"You have no idea what I'm feeling," I said.

"Yes, I do," she said. "I had an equestrian accident in my early twenties. I was paralyzed, and my vocal chords were damaged. I could not swallow or speak, and like you, for a time I had to have a feeding tube. With speech therapy, I regained my voice. I decided then that I wanted to make this my vocation."

How wonderful! They sent me a therapist who understood precisely what I was going through. Her speech sounded perfect. I couldn't hear a hint of the damage she had sustained. This was incredibly inspiring, and it pulled me out of my pity party and restored my positive attitude. Through her, I could see what was possible. The impossible ceased to exist for me.

My case was similar to a stroke victim's. That is, the body cannot perform the functions the mind commands. I formed the words in my mind, and thought I was about to say them, but my muscles refused to cooperate. My tongue did not move.

The fact that I have learned so many different languages helped me in recovering the ability to speak. Fortunately, the surgery had not taken the muscles at the back of my tongue. These are the muscles used to twist and turn the tongue to produce sounds. These subtle movements are called upon to trill the r's in Spanish, for instance. Or make the hard ch sound in German. I believe the varieties of sounds the back of my tongue held in its muscle memory helped speed up the process of relearning to speak.

The therapist and I began by working with vowels. Next we tackled one-syllable words such as mud and food. Then I added two-syllable words such as afraid and three-syllable words such as gingerbread. The letters *s*, *t*, and *p* were most difficult. The *r* is difficult for most people, but I had already trained my tongue to say it in many different ways. The exercises bored me, and I was frustrated with the slow progress. I wanted to utter full sentences right out of the gate, and no way was that going to happen.

My regimen included an amazing array of muscle and throat exercises. I practiced pushing against my tongue, curling, circling, stretching, and puffing my cheeks like a blowfish. I joked to my children that I was performing Pilates with my tongue, and that soon my tongue would perform tricks in Cirque du Soleil. I practiced relentlessly, privately recording myself, listening to my progress or lack of it, and pushing on. It was exhausting.

The speech therapy also retrained my tongue and throat for swallowing and eating. The therapist had a camera that viewed and recorded how I swallowed liquids and ate yogurt. I learned to tuck my chin when swallowing the yogurt and to take small bites. I was forbidden to use a straw and taught to take small sips of liquids. The swallowing exercises had strange names like Bulldog, Masako, Mendelsohn, and Supraglottic.

Like most people, I had always taken swallowing for granted. For most people, it is a reflex, not a carefully orchestrated move. I added the simple ability to swallow to my gratitude list, along with the ability to speak and turn my head and take a walk in the sunshine.

My positive attitude prodded me to try any method that might hasten my recovery. It made common sense to me that I should try to sing, for instance. This would get my voice box moving as well as my tongue. I never had much of an aptitude for singing, but I launched into this new approach to healing with gusto. My alto voice, rough as gravel under a tire, attempted the scales. "Do re mi fa so la ti do," I sang, and Titan scurried to get as far from me as possible.

With plenty of time on my hands, I researched the chemotherapy and radiation I would undergo. The more I read, the more frightened I became. I needed answers to the many questions that arose, and my oncologist, Dr.Eric Nadler, and my radiation oncologist, Dr. Scott Cheek, were happy to oblige.

The purpose of chemo and radiation therapy is to kill all cancer cells left in the body after surgery. Since the lymph nodes route lymph fluid throughout your body, they are also vehicles for harmful substances, and if they are compromised by cancer, they can carry the disease to other organs. This explains why the protocol after surgery calls for chemo and radiation. These therapies kill anything and everything in their paths, and that gives rise to much controversy. If my cancer had not been stage four, I probably would have opted out of chemo and radiation or done a much more limited course of each. That would have been a holistic approach, which many cancer patients are able to choose. Unfortunately, I did not have this option.

Dr. Nadler told me I would be administered Cisplatin for the chemotherapy. It usually does not cause as much nausea and hair loss, as most chemo treatments do, but just in case, he gave me a barrage of medicines for the nausea and instructed me to take the medicines as a preventive measure before it set in. He also prescribed medications for anxiety and sleep.

The chemo treatments sounded like they might be a bit uncomfortable but manageable. The radiation, on the other hand, sounded like a menacing beast. Dr. Cheek and his nurse Katie broke it down for me. The radiation would be comprised of thirty-six treatments. I would have one treatment every weekday that would last fifteen to twenty minutes. On weekends, I would get a break.

I had no illusions about the radiation. There is no way around this extremely difficult procedure, and the doctor did not mince words. During each treatment, my face was covered by a mask made of a pliable white material molded to a perfect fit. I was so appalled at the prospect I barely remember getting fitted. More than ever, I felt I had become a character in a horror show. With the mask placed firmly on my face, I could not see anything. In the complete darkness, I felt I was suffocating. Even though the technicians worked quickly to fashion this contraption for me, I had an anxiety attack, and they had to pause until I recovered. After several attempts, I was finally fitted. After that experience, I knew radiation would take me on a terrifying ride.

The treatments commenced at the end of August. I went down to the Sammons Center at Baylor Hospital on Tuesdays for the chemotherapy. My first few treatments were in a room with several others undergoing chemo. The faces of my fellow patients betrayed a sense of emptiness, as if they had been hollowed out by this disease. Many looked disheveled, uncared for, hopeless, depressed. The sight of them scared me. I was determined not to plunge into that abyss, but sitting in that room, with people who looked like ghosts of their former selves, I feared I could succumb to their hopelessness.

Thanks to my children, I avoided that dark hole of depression. At least one of them came every time and sat with me for the four-hour sessions. Their presence comforted me, and I felt sorry for the patients who did not have the support I did.

As I had been led to expect, the treatment was not so bad. First an anti-nausea medication dripped into my vein, and then the Cisplatin. As soon as the drug entered my system, my mouth dried up. A chill ran through my body and took up residence for the duration of the treatment.

At the end of that first treatment, I thought, This is tolerable. I'm going to fly through this. However, two days later nausea set in. I could barely tolerate water. The shakes repulsed me. The vile liquid that entered my stomach via the feeding tube headed straight for the exit. The bathroom and I began a serious affair.

I wanted only to sleep. The nausea and vomiting tormented me. It didn't take me long to learn to take my anti-nausea meds before the treatments. I still went ahead with the sessions, of course. I had no choice. But days two and three after chemo were always horrible.

The daily radiation treatments began the same week as the chemo. The first week went better than I had expected. The hardest part was my overwhelming dread of the mask. When they put it in place, I could barely see, and each time I experienced the same suffocating claustrophobia that set off an anxiety attack during the fitting. They bolted straps attached to the mask onto the table to keep my head absolutely still. Though I took anxiety medications an hour before, the anxiety never went away entirely. I endured the fright and panic for thirty-six sessions over a twelve-week period.

Except for the terrible anxiety, I didn't mind the radiation that much until the third week. That's when the combination of chemo and radiation began to take its toll on my body. No matter how much medication I took or how far in advance, the nausea set in. I could not fight it. Any stimulation sickened me. Noise, light, and smells tortured me. The television made my head spin. Any noise was too much, even a session with Lupita. The smell of food, perfume, flowers, even soap, caused instant nausea. My favorite perfume made me gag. If Andie washed her hair with a fragrant shampoo, I couldn't bear her tender kisses on my forehead. She kept Titan out of the room after his grooming sessions because they used aromatic products on him. I did not understand why, but my body rejected everything I loved.

I could no longer tolerate the shakes I administered through my feeding tube. I became sicker as the days wore on, and my weight, which I had tried to regain, began to drop. By the fourth week, I was sicker than I had ever been, even before the surgery. My immune system was shot, and I could hold nothing down. The cure was killing me. I could not go through this on my own. In my prayers, I asked God to help me.

One terrible weekend in October, I hit bottom. I could not bear to move. I vomited throughout the day and night, even when I had nothing left to vomit. The medications were powerless against this foe. I wanted to die.

An invisible fire burned my lips, my mouth, my throat. In Barcelona, the heat of the flames in my closet had sent me running for safety. I had opened the window and leapt. Now, all my avenues of escape had shut down. I found myself under a fiery siege. Only sleep brought relief and a sense of peace. When I did sleep, I did not want to wake up to another day of torturous treatments, nausea, pain, utter weakness, and fading hope of recovery.

I began, once again, to question my decision to fight this cancer. No one should have to live this way, even for a day, much less for week after week. Perhaps I had been selfish, unwilling to accept the end of my days. Perhaps the time had come to let go.

Andie saw how much I suffered. She sensed I was losing my grip. Unbeknownst to me, she called Paul and Aina and told them to come to Dallas. She feared I wouldn't make it.

That Monday, Andie took me to the hospital to see my oncologist. By then, I had a fever and I barely had the strength to stand up.

"I am done with this," I said. "I cannot handle these treatments anymore. I would rather die."

My children flew in to be with me. I'm sure they bargained with the devil for my life. And Aina bargained with me. Thinking I was asleep, she sat by my side and made a promise.

"Mumsie, please fight this," she said. "Don't allow this to take you. You have so much still to live for. I promise that if I have a daughter I will name her after you!"

We laugh about this now, but at the time, Aina was really digging deep. Many people in the United States have trouble pronouncing both our names correctly. It's a little burden we carry. She would not have promised to pass this headache on to her child if she had any idea I could hear her. That's how desperate my kids were to see me well again.

The treatments were cancelled for one week while the doctors tried to shore up my strength. They were extremely concerned, but I could not be hospitalized. My white blood cell count had dropped to alarming levels. My weakened immune system couldn't fight off bacteria. They feared I would come down with pneumonia in the hospital, so I stayed at home and went in every day for hydration via an IV.

By the following week, I felt much better. My blood work indicated my immune system had improved. Except for the hydration, I had not been treated medically for the depressed immune system, the fever, the weakness, or the nausea. Nothing had changed except my mind. My work with Lupita addressed my attitude, my motivation. With her help, I was able to let go of the negativity and embrace the positive. By week's end, I was ready to pick myself up and get back into the fight.

We all have a reason to go on living, even when we are longing for an end to our suffering. Yes, in my darkest moment, I wanted to die. Thank God, I had three reasons to live: Paul, Aina, and Andie.

When I truly contemplated death, I knew I was not ready to leave my children. I wanted to see them happily married. I wanted to know their children. I wanted to be there for them, to encourage and motivate them. I wanted to make memories with them. I wanted to give them my self.

During these worst days, my children told me every day, "We are not letting you go. You have to be strong. We know it is tough, but fight it, Mumsie. We need you!"

Their love and support kept me going and gave me strength to fight. More than anything in life, I wanted to be there for them for years to come.

That was not the only time the treatments had to be cancelled. I had to stop them several more times due to weakness and infection. I began referring to radiation as "Dante's Inferno and the Nine Circles of Hell." Every week, the torture intensified. The drugs did nothing to stop the pain or the anxiety. My throat and mouth ached from dryness. I could barely swallow. The radiation and chemo sapped all my strength.

I viewed the torture as a rite of passage from illness to health. No matter how much I suffered, I could not quit. Without these procedures, the cancer would return, and I would die.

Tony Robbins, the motivational speaker, once said, "Whatever you hold in your mind on a consistent basis is exactly what you will experience in your life." That quote became my mantra. I continued to work with Lupita to strengthen my best weapon against cancer—my mind.

From June, when I had the surgery, to the beginning of October, chemo and radiation took over my life. With all the cancellations, the length of the treatment schedule had to be extended. My life became very simple. I went to the hospital for chemo and radiation and returned home and slept. Some days, I slept for fifteen hours. Yes, it was that bad.

Another Tony Robbins quote spoke to me at the time: "Setting goals is the first step in turning the invisible into visible." My goal had been to regain my speech as quickly as possible, and I had devoted myself to the exercises. Sadly, the nausea made it hard to concentrate, and I had to stop my speech therapy. During treatment, staying focused on anything became impossible. I had to set that goal aside for a while. Nevertheless, I stayed grounded and kept my goals in mind, committed to reaching them no matter how things appeared at the moment.

I also cancelled my therapy for the lymphedema, the post-surgery swelling that I was told I would battle for the rest of my life. I have found that, with therapy, it can be controlled, and the swelling can be reduced. I was very committed to the daily therapy regimen, which involved a very light massage in the area to get the liquid flowing. My therapist, Cathy, began working with me soon after the surgery, but once I started the chemo and radiation, I often could not withstand the slightest touch. By the third week of the treatments from hell, I had to take a long break. By then I had developed three chins, and my face had blown up like a balloon. Six months later, I finally felt good enough to do the therapy consistently.

I owe a great deal of my recovery to my amazing children. Their love and support kept me focused on my ultimate goal. I doubt I would be where I am today without them. Every time I stumbled, they took my hand and steadied me. When I was down and hopeless, they picked me up. When the chemo and radiation stole my will to live, they restored it. With the end of treatments in sight, I felt intense gratitude for all three of them.

A few days before Thanksgiving 2015, I underwent my last radiation treatment. It was just as difficult as the thirty-five previous sessions, but I didn't mind. I celebrated the end of torture. When it was finally over, I could not stop smiling. I felt like a conqueror of cancer, the terrible scourge of mankind.

At the Sammons Center, the end of treatment is marked by the banging of a gong. It isn't a very large instrument, but the sound it makes is amplified in the silence inside the depressive atmosphere of that waiting room. Hitting that gong, I felt a tremendous release from the burden of this deadly disease. In the deep ringing sound that echoed through the room, I heard the miracle. I took my place among all those who had walked this terrible path before me and struck that gong in victory. In that room, surrounded by all those who had supported me and nursed me and healed me, I understood what it really meant to be alive. I had survived.

The radiation techs wished me well and gave me the mask as a souvenir of my experience, a symbol of how far I had come. They suggested I create something artistic out of it, as many people do. I had heard of one patient who placed her mask in the haunted house at Six Flags, and I thought that sounded appropriate. After all, radiation and chemo are not unlike going through hell on earth.

For once, I wasn't interested in making art. Not with this mask. I never wanted to see it again. To mark my victory over cancer and the treatments that nearly killed me, I took the mask out to the parking lot and, with great relish, ran over it with my car. The sound of the mask crunching beneath my tire gave me a deeper sense of satisfaction than any work of art I could have made.

7

*A bird sitting on a tree is never afraid of the branch
breaking, because its trust is not on the branch but
on its own wings. Always believe in yourself.*

—Unknown

I spent the Thanksgiving holiday in bed, happy to know
I would not be rising early Monday morning to return
to Sammons for another treatment. I still felt weak and
nauseous, unable to bear the smell of food. I couldn't
cook for my kids. I certainly couldn't enjoy our traditional Thanksgiving feast. Still, I considered it a small
price to pay. This Thanksgiving, I was filled with gratitude for the simple joy of being alive and celebrating with
my children.

I remained isolated from friends, feeling too weak and
still afraid of letting them see my face. I knew it would be

an emotional reunion, and I wasn't ready. Soon, I thought, I will feel up to it. I will return to my old life. This too shall pass.

Unfortunately, the end of treatment did not bring about the happy ending I envisioned. Those who go through radiation refer to it with irony as the gift that keeps on giving. Having survived the invasive therapies, I quickly came to understand the meaning of that phrase.

Radiation eradicates cancer cells, and that is a life-saving gift. However, once the treatments are over, the effects of radiation continue to cause discomfort. Because of radiation, my sense of taste altered dramatically. The weakness and nausea that plagued me during treatment continued for months afterward. My gums hurt, and my burned skin turned various shades of red and blue. So, while radiation gifts you with a new chance at life, it continues giving you things you would rather return. Unfortunately that is not an option. In the next phase of my recovery, it seemed I took one step back for every step forward. I would feel better, and then radiation would leave me another gift. It just kept on surprising me and delivering blows.

In December 2015, I was cleared to start eating. That didn't mean I was ready to sit down to one of the wonderful meals I was accustomed to cooking. I soon learned that eating real food would be another big hurdle on the road to recovery. The first dish I took on was oatmeal. Each spoonful required about twenty minutes to swallow, and the mush felt like sand on my tongue, scraping and scratching my raw throat as I worked to get it down. Texture and the mechanics of swallowing weren't the only problems. Radiation had warped my sense of taste.

I could not even distinguish salt from sweet. Eating, which was always one of the great pleasures of my life, had become an unpleasant, uncomfortable, frustrating chore.

The kids and I thought a change of scene would do me good. Traveling always uplifts me, and I felt ready to manage a short plane ride to San Miguel Allende, where I had spent several months the previous year. We rented a house there for the Christmas holidays, and in late December, I left the scene of my illness and the painful treatments required to survive it. I can't tell you how happy I was to board that plane after all those months trapped in my bed.

On our second evening in San Miguel, we joined a posada, a traditional Mexican celebration that honors Mary and Joseph's search for refuge on the night of Jesus's birth. The fiesta is a gathering of families, neighbors, and strangers passing by. Homes are opened to everyone, and the traditional dishes of the season are offered to all who cross the threshold.

I recalled all the Christmases with my children—the gingerbread houses we made, the Christmas trees they decorated, the torchlight parade of skiers on the mountain in Taos, and Santa Claus's visits. I thought of my girlfriends back in Dallas and the lunches that stretched long into the night. I smiled at the memory of my birthday party, the Frida Kahlo cupcake that prophesied the powers I would marshal in my cancer battle. I thought about the long, lingering dinner with my friend at the Shangri La Hotel in Paris, and how sometimes a celebration is magical even when it is just two women talking, honoring the ups and downs of lives well lived.

The bells of La Parroquia rang, and in the sacred sound, I heard the victory gong at the Sammons Center.

So many celebrations. So many reasons to celebrate. My heart swelled to bursting with the joy of being alive, here, in this enchanting town, walking the posada with family and strangers, all of us celebrating this life we are given.

For eight months I had been a very sick woman. Sometimes I doubted I would survive, and yet, here I was, celebrating another Christmas, very much alive and more than ever in full possession of my self. I couldn't enjoy the holiday fare offered in every home, but I didn't need them. Simply being present was enough.

That Christmas, I enjoyed a renewed appreciation for life and for my relationship with my children. I have to thank cancer for both. With the onset of oral cancer, I lost much of what gave me pleasure. As I slowly regained my ability to do the things I enjoyed, I valued them so much more. As for my children, I had always thought I had a great relationship with them. We loved each other and laughed like families do, but after this ordeal, we became friends.

I saw in each of them the love and compassion they exercised in caring for me. No matter how often I had been told I was a good mom, I never saw it so clearly. I know now that I raised three remarkable human beings. One day they will take care of their families with the same empathy and dedication they displayed toward me.

The new year approached, and I sensed a shift. The nausea receded, and day by day I felt my strength returning. I didn't need as much help accomplishing the simple tasks of daily life. For months I had felt ill around the clock. Then one day I noticed I had four good hours, then six. I began to see the light at the end of the dark tunnel.

I welcomed 2016 in San Miguel. Looking up at the starry sky, I thanked God for giving me strength, hope, love, family, and friends. I felt overwhelmed by all the love that had held me up through my ordeal.

B ack in Dallas, I made my resolution for the new year. I intended to recuperate fully over the next twelve months. Cancer had been one phase. Recovery would be the next. I knew I might never get to where I was before the cancer, but with hard work, I would get close to it. I wanted my life back.

Daily, I attempted a few tasks that brought me closer to independence. I began making trips to the grocery store for the ingredients of my shakes and soups. I just wanted to walk somewhere, to make something with my hands, to build my body back up, make it strong again, capable of doing something useful, something fun.

More than anything, I wanted to have my feeding tube removed. This could only happen once I could take in all my nutrition orally. I feared that day would never come. Sores covered the inside of my mouth. Anything and everything I ingested caused me pain. Brushing my teeth required a sponge and very mild special toothpaste. Liquids were made into puree consistencies so I would not choke. Though I hated the feeding tube, I could not imagine ever eating normally again.

The tube dangled from my waist, and it took constant vigilance to keep it from getting caught up on something. I had to be meticulous about keeping it clean and free of infection. After cleaning it, I reapplied the dressing where it connected to my belly. It took a lot of creativity to keep the lump from showing under my clothes. I embraced wide ponchos, tunics, and kaftans with enthusiasm. But really, I just wanted the tube taken out. It became a major goal in my recovery.

The first step was to begin taking the shakes orally instead of through the tube. Before I could move to that stage, I had to pass a swallowing test, which shows you won't choke or aspirate when you ingest nutrients orally. It is probably difficult to imagine that drinking a milkshake could be so difficult and uncomfortable. My throat was still very raw, and even the smoothest texture felt like sandpaper. My stomach cramped from the effort of digesting the nutrients. Plus, the shakes tasted like steel. I had lost my taste buds in the surgery, and although they are expected to regenerate, my sense of taste at the beginning of 2016 ranged from nonexistent to weird.

I had barely taken any nutrition orally since June 2015. In addition to the shakes, I began to incorporate some creamy soups, but they stung. I was told this was normal and to keep trying. A shake took an hour to swallow. Drinking enough to take in the required two-thousand calories a day left little time for anything else. I would wake up at five o'clock, drink a shake, and go back to sleep until it was time for the next one. In between drinking, I did my therapies. The regimen took over my life.

I applied my culinary creativity to the shakes and soups, experimenting with ingredients, proportions, and textures to no avail. They tasted horrible. After about two weeks, I tolerated the shakes. My body and taste buds accepted the soups gradually and inconsistently. What worked for me one day didn't the next. For six weeks I ignored the pain and discomfort and drank my two thousand calories. My weight stabilized, and I had not used my feeding tube. I was homing in on my goal.

I crossed that finish line on Valentine's Day. Hallelujah! The feeding tube was removed. In my old life, I enjoyed receiving flowers and candies on this holiday. But this year, I was ecstatic about this one gift: I no longer had this alien contraption protruding from my waist. I had also missed sleeping on my stomach. It's funny how we take little comforts like that for granted.

Slowly, I incorporated soft solids. My new tongue had to learn to receive the messages from my brain to send the food down my throat. As I write, in the autumn of 2016, this task is still challenging, but I have experienced much improvement. I hadn't realized how many signals are involved in eating. One day I watched a woman eat an apple as she walked her dog. Before the surgery I, too, had this ability to "walk and chew gum at the same time." But now, I have to concentrate when I eat. Talking while eating is not possible. It's just too exhausting. For a long time, I felt embarrassed to dine with my friends, because it took me so long to eat, and I couldn't join in the conversation. With practice and patience my tongue is learning how to manage the simple task of sending food down my throat without my constant vigilance. I look forward to the day when I will be back in my kitchen, throwing a beautiful dinner together for my friends, raising a toast, and celebrating life with a feast.

The food challenge was just one of many obstacles I had to overcome. My recovery took on the characteristics of a major post-war operation. Just as the Marshall Plan was developed to rebuild Europe after World War II, I had to create a strict regimen to rebuild my health.

Every head and neck patient that gets radiation develops excessive mucous for a couple of months after treatment. It is another "gift" of radiation. Besides making me nauseous, the mucus interfered with my speech. What was already difficult became even more so with the sticky gunk in my throat. The more I cleared it, the faster it returned. If I had known, I would have bought stock in a tissue company. For several months I supported my drug store, purchasing six to eight boxes a day. Some people use towels, but that's just not my style.

I was also determined to get off all opiates. Under my doctor's supervision, I began to wean myself. For the first time in my life, I knew exactly what a person hooked on drugs must feel like. Letting go of the painkillers showed me how much they had helped in keeping me relatively comfortable. I would have preferred not to feel the pain, but I knew these were signals from my body. It was adjusting to changes such as my neck's immobility and the assaults of the chemo and radiation. Meditation helped tremendously in this effort. Staying in the present, saying yes to the suffering as well as the pleasures of any given moment, kept me from staying stuck in the pain. Gradually, by accepting it instead of fighting it, it moved on as all things do. It took me two weeks to get completely off all medication. It wasn't easy, and I felt proud of myself for freeing myself so quickly. The only pills I continued to take were vitamins in capsules that easily slid down my throat; any other form was not possible.

The human body is a complex, intricate instrument. For the system to function, every part has to do its job and work in concert with other parts. After my illness, I came to a new appreciation of my body. Imagine. Medicine has come so far that I got a new tongue. I felt tremendous gratitude for this miracle of science as well as the back muscle that was left intact. This made it possible to recover the nerve messages and muscle memories required to speak and eat.

Over a period of weeks, I started exercising more. In the beginning, I was exhausted after walking for ten minutes. Sticking with a daily routine, I gradually increased my exercise time. Soon, I didn't require a nap after exerting myself a little.

Getting well became my full-time job. I had no interest in anything that didn't further my goal to enjoy the activities that filled my days before the whole cancer drama.

I needed to do things on my own and I longed to take care of my children again, as I always had. I wanted to be their mother again. My children's support throughout my illness meant the world to me, but it was time to reverse our roles again.

I told my children they should go back home. At first they refused, but I insisted. The time had come to go solo. "I appreciate all you've done for me," I said, "but I can take it from here." They kept coming back for weekends and planning to extend their stays into the following week, but I shook my head and said no. "You need to go home now. I can handle it on my own. I didn't survive chemo and radiation to end up bedridden or unable to take care of myself. To get stronger, I have to stop being spoon-fed. I have to do things on my own." They obeyed me with great reluctance, and though I knew it was for the best, I missed them terribly.

Taking care of myself was a challenge, but I loved regaining my independence. I limited my errands to one a day plus my therapies. My speed dial had the number of every restaurant, grocery store, and drug store that delivered. A housekeeper came every day to help out, and of course, I had my very loving friends, who would do anything I asked.

I had often heard that people stick around for a couple of weeks after a major illness or tragedy, and then they gradually vanish. I did not have this experience. My friends have been with me every step of the way. They visited when I truly wanted no one, but I appreciated their constancy. They helped my kids when I was weak and couldn't be much of a mother. Even when I couldn't see anyone, they were there for me.

My friends called me regularly, and though it was difficult to understand me, especially at first, they told me how good I sounded. Little did they know how hard won those short conversations were. I practiced for hours every day and recorded myself in order to measure my improvement. It would have been easy to become complacent. I still experienced a lot of pain. There were plenty of excuses not to do my therapies. But I didn't allow myself that weakness. I had goals to reach. And soon.

My journey taught me that positive attitude is key in overcoming adversity. Without it, everything else you do is less effective. Meditation may be the most important tool in my kit. Through my daily practice, I nurtured my positive attitude and learned to let the negative go. During my illness, I meditated each morning and night, and I continue to do so. Just ten minutes makes me feel centered and at peace. Meditation brought me clarity and grounded me even during this challenging time. Thanks to my faith, I could trust in the unknown, and thanks to meditation, I developed the patience to see miracles evolve in my life.

I found I had to be patient with myself. It was all well and good to have motivation and goals, but I had to rein myself in and remember to take one step at a time. I learned that consistency is more effective than speed. I progressed faster taking shorter walks every day than I did if I overextended myself and ended up back in bed for two days.

That's not to say I didn't push myself. I had to. There were times that my soul stayed strong, but my body wasn't willing to go along with the program. I had to force myself to do my exercises, take that walk, swallow one more shake. The little tasks I accomplished became bigger ones, and soon I found myself closing in on goals I hadn't been so sure I could reach. For me, it boiled down to hard work and patience. Sometimes I didn't walk as far as I had the day before or a phone conversation went badly, and I wanted to beat myself up. Most times, I resisted that temptation. I rose up and kept walking. I stayed true to my promise that a better me was in the making.

Isolation is the enemy of recovery. It is bad for the mind, body, and soul. I had to go out even when I didn't feel up to it, and push myself to accept invitations. I felt embarrassed about my new face—the red and purple skin, burned from the radiation, and the lymphedema that swelled me up. Sometimes it felt much easier just to stay at home. But there is so much to enjoy on the other side of my front door and so much opportunity for growth and healing. Every time I braved an outing, it became easier. Being around others helped me see how far I had come, especially among my friends, who gave me honest feedback about my progress.

I felt eager to return to my art. My oil paints, brushes, and canvases lay dormant since well before the surgery, and I longed to begin again. I expected the cancer would inspire me to become more prolific, since tragedy seems to bring out the best in creative minds. I was so excited the first time I opened my kit and set up my easel. Then the smell of the oil paints hit me, and I received yet another gift from radiation: the paints made me sick. It killed me to forego painting, which I had come to love. I tried using acrylics, but they didn't inspire me. Sadly, I put my paints away, looking forward to the day when I could do my art again.

I couldn't paint, but after the long drought during chemo and radiation, I could read again. Thirsty for knowledge, I delved into anything I could lay my hands on. I read as if I had been banished from books for a lifetime. During my recovery, I had the time to rediscover the life of the mind.

My energy work with Lupita and spiritual seeking have remained central to my life. I have found that understanding and enlightenment come gradually as we open ourselves to new possibilities, relinquish old patterns, and develop a deep intimacy with ourselves.

In my spiritual work, I developed the habit of gratitude. It plays a major role in nurturing my positive attitude and, consequently, in my renewal. Even when I was a long way from complete physical recovery, I was somehow content and extremely grateful. Every time I succeeded in saying a new word clearly or eating a bite of something I hadn't been able to swallow before, I felt gratitude. And each moment of gratitude moved me a little further along in my healing. Gratitude keeps us from succumbing to negativity as it invites miracles into our lives. I am eternally grateful for my journey and all the blessings I continue to have despite cancer.

It's easy to forget to express our gratitude to those we love. I thought I had always told my loved ones how much I adored them, but now, expressing my love and admiration takes on new importance. Today, I don't say, "I love you," out of habit. "I love you too," is no longer an automatic response. I feel a sense of urgency about sharing my feelings. I know now that we never know how much time we have left. Death comes knocking on its own schedule.

Time seems to have stretched since my illness. There is no longer any reason to rush. I have all the time in the world to be a good friend, to stop and listen. Through this journey I have learned that listening is an art. It's easy to slip into lazy listening—thinking about how we want to reply rather than hearing what someone has to say. When I lost my ability to speak, I learned to listen. Without this tragedy, I don't know when I would have learned when to offer advice to my family and friends and when to simply listen.

I appreciate every day as the gift it truly is. I smile at the wonders of the world—the rain and the sun and the rainbows they make together. Cancer awakened me from my slumber and cast everything in a bright, new, beautiful light.

I stepped out on my balcony one morning and felt a change in the air. A bright green haze blanketed the red oaks and pecans in the park below. Overnight, the trees had budded. Birds flitted to and fro, busy building their nests and feeding their young. With the arrival of spring, my one-year anniversary was right around the corner. I laughed out loud thinking back to the day in May when the doctor's diagnosis had struck fear in my heart. I thought of how sad I had been, how hopeless I had felt. I had no idea then of my inner strength or the powerful positive attitude I would develop to fight this disease. Cancer made me stronger. It taught me what I am capable of. It took me to great heights, and from this vantage point, I laughed with a joy and love for life I had never known.

One day in March 2016, I walked into the Sammons Cancer Center for a scan. I felt confident it would show I was healed. A couple of days later the results validated my optimism. The doctor pronounced me cancer-free.

In your face, cancer! I showed up, I endured, and I conquered you!

As I write this, it has been less than two years since the end of my treatments, and I have already reached most of the goals I set for myself. I have managed to speak quite clearly. Some days are better than others, and I see consistent improvement. Just hearing my own voice makes me happy. Having a conversation, telling my story to an audience, calling my children on the phone—these are miraculous achievements.

I take pride in my body and work out three to four times a week to stay in shape. With strength training, walking, and using a stationary bicycle, I am stronger now than I was before I got sick.

For over a year, I had daily lymphedema therapy and wore a custom-fitted mask ten hours a day. In December 2016, I began to use a pneumatic compression device, newly developed by Flexitouch for head and neck cancer patients. It looks like scuba gear and acts as a pump to move the fluid out. Now I do this treatment for thirteen to thirty-two minutes a day, and my lymphedema is remarkably improved. Only a small bump below my chin remains.

I finally found a treatment to remove the ugly spots from the radiation burns on my neck: Soothe, by Rodan and Fields. I always had great skin, but it took a beating from radiation and chemo. Now, after trying countless creams and potions, I found that the Rodan and Fields has restored the healthy glow in my face, and my neck is almost where I desire. The great skin I inherited from my mother is back.

When I look in the mirror today, I see the new me, the Ilse who beat cancer. The old Ilse is gone. I don't grieve over what is lost. I have found, instead, a better me. The changes in me are not imperfections. They are the perfect signs of the challenge I have overcome.

My ability to eat solid foods continues to improve, though I still struggle with certain foods. A regimen of supplements called Juice Plus fulfills my nutritional needs for fruits and vegetables that I cannot eat, and I have continued to add it to my diet. I'm enjoying my sweetheart espressos again, one of the great pleasures of life. At parties, I can have a glass of wine or water with vodka. Yes—I can finally drink a glass of wine or champagne without watering it down!

Every day brings improvement and with it, hope. I look forward to my bright future, and I hear myself saying bon appétit as my friends and family sit down with me to a wonderful meal. In my vision, I raise a glass of bubbly and make a toast to health, to love, to life.

I have been relentless at getting better and regaining the quality of life I enjoyed before cancer. Everything takes time. Every day ushers in a new chance at life. Each morning when I wake, I am filled with gratitude for this world and my place in it. Life is, indeed, wonderful.

In Memoriam

Titan passed away on October 3, 2016. He was my loyal companion for fourteen years. Through good times and bad, he never left my side, but he was tired, and it was past time for him to go. I am convinced he held on until he saw me recovered. He died in my arms, and I will miss him forever.

Epilogue
A Note to Fellow Travelers

The life in front of you is far more important than the life behind you.

—Joel Osteen

We cancer survivors are a tight-knit community, and we don't hesitate to reach out to newcomers. I never turn down an opportunity to talk with people who are facing treatments for oral cancer or similar challenges. If someone had shared their experience with me, many of my fears might have been alleviated. No one can explain what you are about to go through as well as someone who has gone through it.

Sharing my story helps others and contributes to my healing as well. As I talk about the surgery, the radiation, the chemo, and the months of recovery, I realize how far I have come. Writing this book is another form of sharing and giving back. Perhaps in the details of my challenges and how I overcame them, readers will find the inspiration and courage to face their own.

An important part of my story is the loving support I got from my family. Many cancer patients relapse because they have no one rooting for them. No one is pushing them to fight the battle another day. Some lose their will to continue fighting because they have no one to love. They feel there is no one to hold on to and no reason to live. If you are a cancer patient, stay connected to friends and loved ones. Don't give in to the temptation to isolate. If you don't have a person to love, love a pet. Give yourself love in your life. You will need it when the pain hits you, and you feel like quitting. A loving relationship makes you determined to battle the suffering another day. In the midst of it all, I knew I had many feasts yet to share, many glasses yet to raise in celebration, many memories to make with loved ones. That is how I said *no* to cancer.

Cancer is not healed by medicine alone. Doctors and their treatments can only do so much. Without a positive attitude, those treatments often fail: the healing doesn't progress; the body relapses. A positive attitude sets the pace for your healing. From the outset, even the mention of cancer strikes fear in a patient's heart, and there begins the spiral downward to a gloomy, hopeless place. The body may survive, but the soul becomes weak and irreparable.

Yes, cancer is scary, but it is not a death sentence if you have a life worth fighting for. There is no need to be frightened or to give in to hopelessness. When I was diagnosed, I couldn't keep from asking God why this oral cancer happened to me. I couldn't squelch my anger and deep frustration at the injustice of it. These reactions are natural, but they are not useful. If the soul is weak, how can it nurture the body? True healing begins in our souls. Inner strength is essential to the healing of the body.

A cancer diagnosis is a shock, no doubt about it. Let yourself have a pity party if you must, but not for long.

Move on to positivity and acceptance. That's how you become strong enough to fight for your life. There will be times when you fall back into negativity. I certainly did. During radiation, I became so weak in body and soul that I wanted to slip away. I wanted to surrender to death, but my soul waxed stronger and pushed negative thoughts away. I told myself, I will survive, and I focused on overcoming every challenge cancer threw at me. I persisted.

Persistence is critical in a battle like this. Never quit trying. I have done exceptionally well in my recovery from oral cancer. I attribute this success to my unwillingness to give up. Ever. I kept moving forward. I thought of the life I wanted to live after cancer. I didn't want to spend my days in a wheelchair or in bed. I wanted to speak clearly again, indulge in my love of food and cooking, paint, dance with my friends, and take care of my future grandchildren.

I have reached many of the goals for recovery I set out for myself. Others are within my grasp. I didn't get here by giving in to sorrow over my losses and fears of my future. I got here because I had an attitude: I said *yes* to life!

Acknowledgments

I want to thank my charming team of gardeners who assisted me in developing, pruning, and bringing to blossom my book *Say Yes to Life*. Cindy Birne led the charge, followed by my editor, Barbara Norris, who helped me unravel many layers of this profound experience to tell "my story," and Omar Mediano, my talented artistic director, photographer, cover designer, website designer, and social media coordinator. I am very lucky to have this extraordinarily talented team behind me, and the support and enthusiasm of my new friends.

I am eternally grateful to my doctors, Dr. Lance Oxford, MD, Dr. Eric S. Nadler, MD, Dr. Scott Cheek, MD, and Dr. Jason Potter, MD, who gave me a second chance at life by utilizing their medical expertise on me. You are rock stars every step of the way!

My gratitude goes to Brad Smith and Cathy Reed in the Lymphedema and Speech Department at Baylor University Medical Center at Dallas, Bonnie Lucio in Physical Therapy, and Katie Bukholt in Radiation Oncology, also at Baylor University Medical Center at Dallas. Though I hated every treatment in radiation and chemotherapy, the kindness and patience shown towards me—by every nurse and technician—was always present. Thank you!

Namaste to Lupita Gurulé dé Martinéz for making me recapture *me*, and for helping me regain my soul.

My love and many *muchas gracias* and *besos*, to my *amigas* who stood strong by my side, building a wall of love and compassion that helped me in more ways than they will ever know.

Thank you to all of my dear friends, who are too many to name individually, yet you each hold a very special place in my heart. Thank you. *Muchas gracias. Merci!*

Thank you to Dr. Eric S. Nadler, MD, Sergio Nicolau, Cathy Brittingham Saxon, Rebecca Koven, Kristin S. Kaufman, and Lupita Gurulé dé Martinéz, who were kind enough to contribute commendations for this book.

You would not be reading *Say Yes to Life* were it not for my publisher, Larry Carpenter, who provided knowledge and years of experience in the publishing sector. Thank you!

To my three gems ... and Titan. I love you forever to the moon and back!

To Cancer: you didn't stand a chance against my above team and me. In spite of you I wrote *Say Yes to Life*!